KNIT LIKE A

Latvian

...SOCKS

50 knitting patterns for knee-length socks, ankle socks and leg warmers

Ieva Ozolina

DAVID & CHARLES

www.davidandcharles.com

Contents

Introduction

Dear knitting enthusiast, thank you for choosing my book!

Latvia is a small country located in Northern Europe, by the Baltic Sea, smaller than Scotland and with less than half as many inhabitants. The damp and windy coastal climate has always created a need for warm clothing, which is why Latvia is steeped in a rich heritage of knitting traditions.

The first records of knitting in Latvia date back to the 13th century, but we suspect that Latvians have knitted for much longer than that.

Every region in Latvia has its own unique way of knitting socks. Winter socks were knitted using sheep's wool and summer socks from linen or cotton. The socks weren't only necessary for warmth, but were also worn as an accessory and a form of expression.

Socks for daily use were bright and made with wool. For practical reasons they were a solid colour at the bottom of the foot because this part deteriorated the fastest and had to be reknitted.

In ancient times, yarns were dyed with natural, plant-based pigments, using ingredients like roots, flowers and even mushrooms to colour the wool.

Women complemented their clothing with stockings that were decorated with traditional symbols and colourful patterns, both partially and all over the sock. Particularly elegant were the lace stockings for women.

I have been looking for samples of authentic socks all over Latvia and have had help from the Ethnographic Open-Air Museum of Latvia, Madona Local History and Art Museum, Kuldiga District Museum and Liepaja Museum, who all kindly agreed to share their carefully preserved historical collections with me.

However, this is not a history book. This is a practical knitting book in which I have combined Latvian knitting traditions with a modern perspective and application.

I hope you find your perfect pair of Latvian socks within this book.

Good luck!

Ieva

SYMBOLS GUIDE

Here are some of the most common symbols featured in Latvian sock patterns, with an explanation of their meaning.

THE SIGN OF GOD

In ancient Latvian mythology, God was not just the father of the Gods, he was the essence of them all. This symbol represents the sky, as a roof over the Earth.

THE SIGN OF MĀRA

The deity of earth and water and all the creatures within. Māra is the protector of women, especially mothers, and children. She is goddess of the Earth.

THE SIGN OF LAIMA

Goddess of destiny. Laima determined the destiny of people. The name Laima derives from the word laime, which means "happiness" or "luck". The sign is thought to bring luck.

THE SIGN OF THE STAR

The star protects from evil. The simplest form of star is a basic cross shape, created by lines crossing at right angles, which symbolises fire and the light. A cross in Latvian folklore has six or eight stars and is one of the only surviving symbols to still honour the winter ceremonies and celebrations.

THE SIGN OF AUSEKLIS (MORNING STAR)

The usher of the new day. Auseklis is thought to protect people from the forces of evil that roam at night.

THE SIGN OF THE SUN

The Sun is the dominant feature of God's heaven. The Sun is the goddess of fertility, and also the patron goddess of the unlucky. The sign of the Sun is the most frequently used element in Latvian design.

THE CROSS OF MĀRA (CROSS OF CROSSES)

Related to fire, home and productivity (fertility). It guards, blesses and brings happiness.

ZALKTIS (SERPENT)

Zalktis was the guardian of wealth and well-being, and therefore had to be protected and cared for. Zalktis was thought to be a sacred animal, and had access to worldwide knowledge. The sign of Zalktis symbolises wisdom, ancient arts and sacred crafts.

TOOLS AND MATERIALS

NEEDLES

In ancient times sock knitters used tiny metal needles, but now we have so many options: steel, aluminium, bamboo, resin or wood. Any of these are suitable for sock knitting and you can use your preferred option.

We traditionally use five double pointed needles for knitting Latvian socks, and all the socks and stockings shown in this book have been knitted with double pointed needles ranging in size from 1.5–3.5mm.

For knitting some stockings, we used 2 or 3 different needle sizes to create the leg shaping, using larger needles for the calf and smaller ones for the ankle and foot.

YARN

Natural, 100% wool, 2-ply wool is traditionally used for Latvian socks and stockings. This is the best choice for knitting authentic socks, because this yarn is most similar to hand-spun yarn, which was used in ancient times. Another reason to use wool yarns is the huge range of colours available.

Most socks and some of the stockings are knitted with 2-ply 100% wool (350m per 100g).

If you prefer more modern options, you can knit with 4-ply sock yarn (75% wool, 25% polyamide) (400m per 100g). This yarn is similar in thickness and is much softer, more durable and flexible, which makes socks or stockings last much longer.

Some of socks in this book are knitted with 6-ply sock yarn (375m per 150g).

Each pattern provides information on the number of colours used, including the base colour.

For most socks with a coloured leg or cuff, the foot is worked in the base colour and total amounts required will depend upon the length of the foot and the leg.

For the main base colour of each pair of short socks or leg warmers you will need: approximately 50–75g of base colour, plus approximately 25g for each additional colour. Note that for some projects not all of the 25g of any additional colours will be used.

For longer socks you will need 100–150g of base colour.

Use each chart as a guide for using colours – each square on the chart represents one stitch to be worked in the yarn colour indicated.

These amounts are intended as a general guide only.

OTHER EQUIPMENT

- A thin elastic or rubber thread can be knitted into the cuff for a better fit and to help to keep the stockings up.

- A strong linen, hemp or nylon thread can be knitted into the heels to make them stronger. This is recommended if you knit with pure wool yarn.

- A pair of sharp scissors for snipping yarn.

- A hard, see-through ruler for measuring tension (gauge).

- A tape measure for measuring the length of longer pieces of knitting.

- A blunt-ended tapestry/wool needle (a pointy needle will split the yarn and spoil your knitting).

- A cable needle for some of the more complex stitches.

- Rust proof pins with glass heads (for visibility) for measuring your tension.

- Sock blockers for blocking your work.

- Stitch markers to indicate the start of the round, or to mark a pattern repeat.

- Row counter to keep a note of how many rows or rounds you've knitted.

- Notebook and pen, as an alternative to a row counter, or to make notes of your tension or any alterations or adaptations you make to a pattern.

- Project bag for keeping your work and equipment in.

Follow the steps below to knit your socks.

1. Read the Tools and Materials section, which specifies the type of yarn required and recommended needle size.

2. Check your tension following the instructions below and make a note of the needle size you need to use to achieve the required tension. To maintain tension with Fair Isle knitting you may need to change to a larger needle size for stocking (stockinette) stitch Fair Isle or to a smaller needle size for garter stitch Fair Isle.

3. Choose your sock, stocking or leg warmer pattern.

4. Choose your yarn and colours, making sure you have enough of each colour (see Yarn).

5. Cast on the required number of stitches as specified in your chosen pattern and work the required cuff, following the instructions in the Basic Sock Recipe section.

6. Continue to work your sock following the Basic Sock Recipe and the chart(s) provided. If one chart is given you will need to repeat it as stated. If two charts are given, one will run on from the other.

7. Block your socks before wearing as this will neaten up your stitches and make your patterns really stand out (see Blocking your Projects).

CHECKING YOUR TENSION (GAUGE)

Before starting your socks you will need to knit a tension (gauge) swatch.

Slightly looser socks are recommended so that you can move your toes inside the socks freely – if your socks are too tight or a little too small, they won't feel comfortable.

Your knitted swatch will need to mirror the circular knitting of the socks and cannot be knitted flat as your tension will not be the same compared to when knitting in the round. This is because when you work stocking stitch in the round only knit stitches are used, whereas when you work stocking stitch flat in rows, both knit and purl stitches are used. Tension can be different when knitting these two stitches, so they can vary slightly in size and can also use different amounts of yarn.

The patterns in this book include a couple of short ankle warmer variations (Dagda and Balvi Leg Warmers), so we recommend that you choose a pair of these to knit first in order to check your tension.

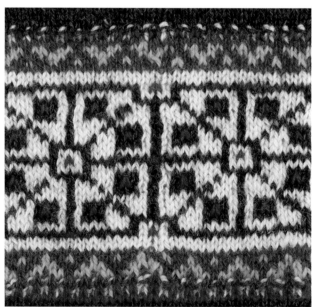

HOW TO MEASURE TENSION

1. Lay your knitted leg warmer on a flat surface. Place a see-through ruler vertically across the top and measure 5cm (2in) across the centre. Mark the beginning and end of the 5cm (2in) length with pins.

2. Do the same vertically and place pins as markers.

3. Count how many stitches and how many rounds there are between the pins. To maintain an even tension over both plain knitting and Fair Isle knitting, you may need to change needle sizes whilst you work, otherwise your socks may be too tight.

The correct tension to achieve when using 2-ply wool or 4-ply sock yarn is:

3.25 sts and 4 rows per cm (32.5 sts and 40 rows per 10cm). Try using needles between 2-2.5mm, and if needed, try 2.75mm. Make a note of which needle sizes you need for each stitch type and use these throughout.

Once you have found the correct needle sizes for your tension, if desired you can use one needle size larger for the fairisle sections to make a looser cuff.

For 6-ply yarn, tension to achieve for stocking stitch is:

2.7 sts and 3.4 rows per cm (27 sts and 34 rows per 10cm). Try using needles between 3-3.5mm.

If your stitch and round counts are the same as specified above, you can go ahead and start knitting. If you have more stitches and rounds, you are knitting too tightly and you project will end up too small. You'll need to make another swatch with slightly larger needles and measure again.

If you have fewer stitches than specified, you are knitting too loosely and your project will be too big. You'll need to make another pair of leg warmers with slightly smaller needles and measure again.

Continue to swatch with different sized needles until you achieve the correct tension stated.

If your tension (gauge) testing results in a few pairs of leg warmers that are too big or too small for your legs, then you can give them away as gifts.

READING CHARTS

- Each square on the chart represents one stitch.

- Knit or purl each stitch in the colour shown on the chart.

- Read all charts from right to left. Where one chart is provided, repeat the chart twice for each sock. Where two charts are provided, follow the right-hand chart first, then follow the left-hand chart for each sock.

- Where a heel or toe chart is provided separately, follow these for the heel and toe patterns.

- For full details on the cuff method used, read the Basic Sock Recipe

- For some socks, sloping sections of heel or toe charts represent the decreases for flat toes and flat heels.

- Where the chart reduces in width by one square, this indicates a decrease of one stitch for each pattern repeat; where the chart increases in width by one square, this indicates an increase of one stitch for each pattern repeat.

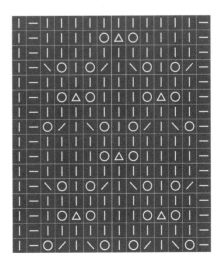

Projects

The patterns begin with ankle socks, followed by knee-length socks and leg warmers. Difficulty levels vary, with the more difficult or complex patterns using more than two colours of yarn in one round. It you're new to working in the round, you may wish to start with a simpler pattern that uses two colours only.

- Don't forget to refer to the Basic Sock Recipe for the full instructions for cuff, heel, gusset and toe.

- Remember that each square of the chart represents a stitch to be worked in the colour indicated.

- Charts are read from the bottom up, and the red line indicates the halfway point in the pattern.

WHITE STAR

Notes

Refer to Basic Sock Recipe for full instructions.

3 colours of yarn used: base colour (black), and 2 contrast colours (orange and cream).

2–2.5mm needles and 2-ply wool.

1. Cast on 72 sts with base colour.

2. Divide equally between 4 needles on first round (18 sts per needle).

3. Work cuff following The Notches method (see Cuff Techniques).

4. Continue with leg, following chart pattern. Read chart from right to left and repeat chart twice.

5. Continue with base colour only and work 30 rounds straight.

6. Work heel with base colour, noting the variation in location of right and left heel flaps, as the heel part of each sock is knitted on different needles (see Basic Sock Recipe).

7. Work gusset with base colour.

8. Work foot with base colour.

9. Work toe with base colour, following Banded Toe Cap and Finishing method (see Basic Sock Recipe).

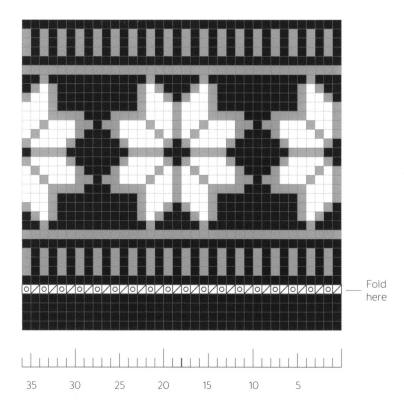

Fold here

35 30 25 20 15 10 5

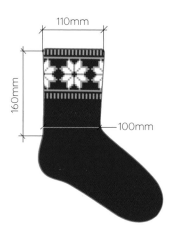

110mm

160mm

100mm

(Designed with reference to museum exhibit no: BDM Nr.4281, Limbaži. Apr.1930th)

BRIGHT STAR

Notes

Refer to Basic Sock Recipe for full instructions.

5 colours of yarn used: base colour (cream), and 4 contrast colours (navy blue, yellow, burnt orange and green).

2–2.5mm needles and 2-ply wool.

1. Cast on 72 sts with base colour.

2. Divide equally between 4 needles on first round (18 sts per needle).

3. Work cuff following The Notches method (see Cuff Techniques).

4. Continue with leg, following chart pattern. Read chart from right to left and repeat twice.

5. With base colour, work a further 8 rounds straight.

6. Work heel with base colour, noting the variation in location of right and left heel flaps (see Basic Sock Recipe).

7. Work gusset with base colour.

8. Work foot with base colour.

9. Work toe with base colour, following Banded Toe Cap and Finishing method (see Basic Sock Recipe).

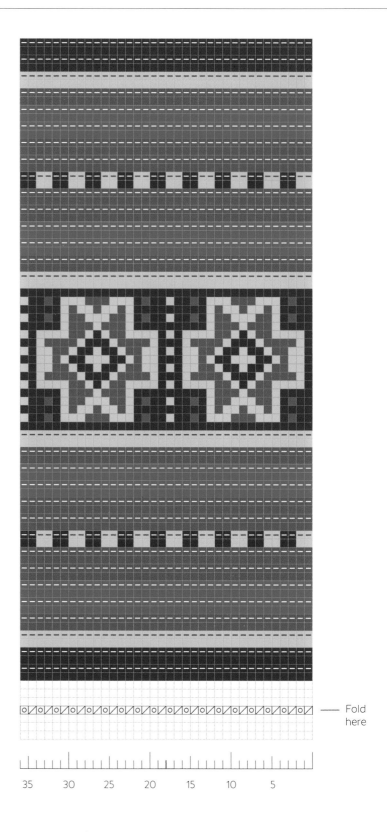

Fold here

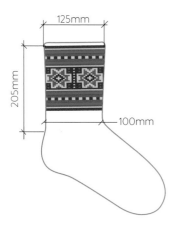

125mm

205mm

100mm

(Designed with reference to museum exhibit no: KNM 3179)

ALPEN ROSE

Notes

Refer to Basic Sock Recipe for full instructions.

5 colours of yarn used: base colour (white), and 4 contrast colours (purple, pink, red and mustard).

2–2.5mm needles and 2-ply wool.

1. Cast on 72 sts with base colour.

2. Divide equally between 4 needles on first round (18 sts per needle).

3. Work cuff following The Notches method (see Cuff Techniques).

4. Continue with leg, following chart pattern. Read chart from right to left and repeat twice.

5. Work heel with base colour, noting the variation in location of right and left heel flaps (see Basic Sock Recipe).

6. Work gusset with base colour.

7. Work foot with base colour.

8. Work toe with base colour, following Rounded Toe Cap and Finishing method (see Basic Sock Recipe).

Fold here

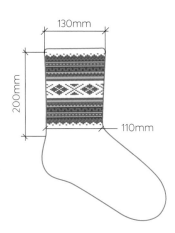

AUTUMN

Notes

Refer to Basic Sock Recipe for full instructions.

5 colours of yarn used: base colour (pale grey), and 4 contrast colours (burgundy, mustard, navy blue and light brown).

2–2.5mm needles and 2-ply wool.

1. Cast on 72 sts with base colour.

2. Divide equally between 4 needles on first round (18 sts per needle).

3. Work cuff following The Notches method (see Cuff Techniques).

4. Continue with leg, following chart pattern, working Latvian braids where indicated (see Cuff Techniques). Read chart from right to left and repeat twice.

5. Work heel with base colour, noting the variation in location of right and left heel flaps (see Basic Sock Recipe).

6. Work gusset with base colour.

7. Work foot with base colour.

8. Work toe with base colour, following Rounded Toe Cap and Finishing method (see Basic Sock Recipe).

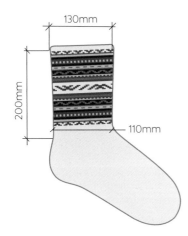

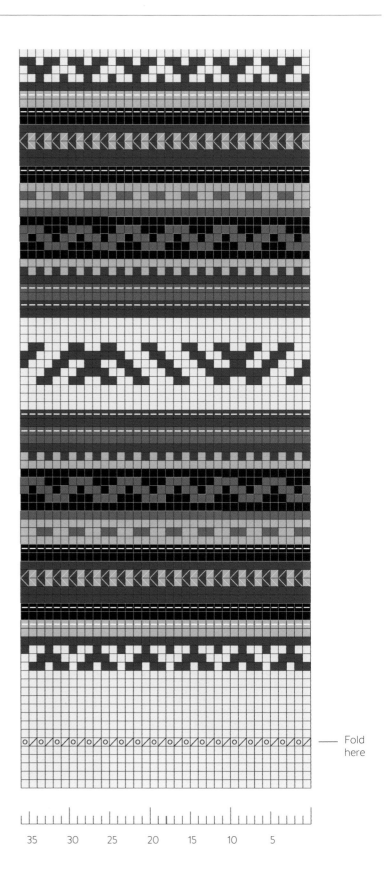

Fold here

35   30   25   20   15   10   5

CORNFLOWER

Notes

Refer to Basic Sock Recipe for full instructions.

5 colours of yarn used: base colour (grey), and 4 contrast colours (navy blue, light blue, white and green).

2–2.5mm needles and 2-ply wool.

1. Cast on 72 sts with base colour.

2. Divide equally between 4 needles on first round (18 sts per needle).

3. Work cuff following The Notches method (see Cuff Techniques).

4. Continue with leg, following chart pattern. Read chart from right to left and repeat twice.

5. With base colour, work a further 2 rounds straight.

6. Work heel with base colour, noting the variation in location of right and left heel flaps (see Basic Sock Recipe).

7. Work gusset with base colour.

8. Work foot with base colour.

9. Work toe with base colour, following Rounded Toe Cap and Finishing method (see Basic Sock Recipe).

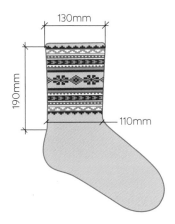

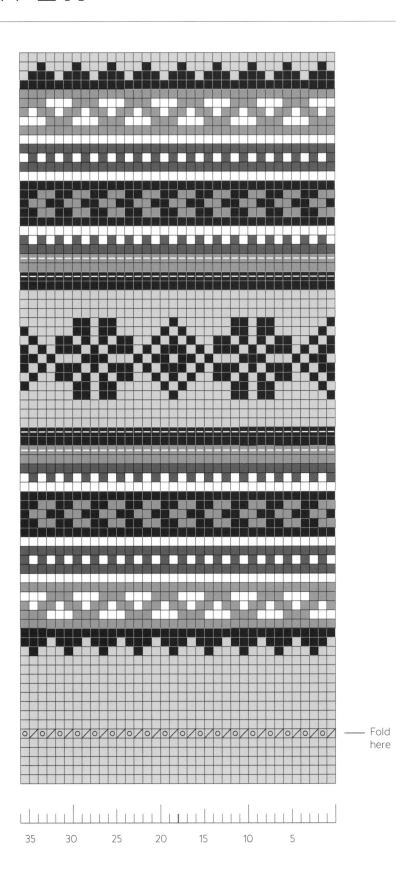

Fold here

SUNFLOWER

Notes

Refer to Basic Sock Recipe for full instructions.

5 colours of yarn used: base colour (grey), and 4 contrast colours (yellow, burgundy, beige and brown).

2–2.5mm needles and 2-ply wool.

1. Cast on 72 sts with base colour.

2. Divide equally between 4 needles on first round (18 sts per needle).

3. Work cuff following The Notches method (see Cuff Techniques).

4. Continue with leg, following chart pattern. Read chart from right to left and repeat twice.

5. Work heel with base colour, noting the variation in location of right and left heel flaps (see Basic Sock Recipe).

6. Work gusset with base colour.

7. Work foot with base colour.

8. Work toe with base colour, following Rounded Toe Cap and Finishing method (see Basic Sock Recipe).

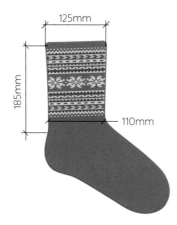

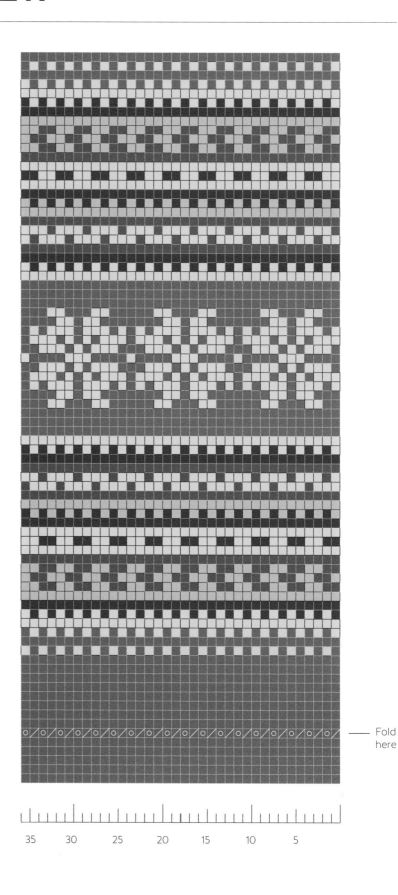

Fold here

35 30 25 20 15 10 5

POPPY

Notes

Refer to Basic Sock Recipe for full instructions.

5 colours of yarn used: base colour (black), and 4 contrast colours (red, green, yellow and navy blue).

2–2.5mm needles and 2-ply wool.

1. Cast on 72 sts with base colour.

2. Divide equally between 4 needles on first round (18 sts per needle).

3. Work cuff following The Notches method (see Cuff Techniques).

4. Continue with leg, following chart pattern. Read chart from right to left and repeat twice.

5. With base colour, work a further 3 rounds straight.

6. Work heel with base colour, noting the variation in location of right and left heel flaps (see Basic Sock Recipe).

7. Work gusset with base colour.

8. Work foot with base colour.

9. Work toe with base colour, following Rounded Toe Cap and Finishing method (see Basic Sock Recipe).

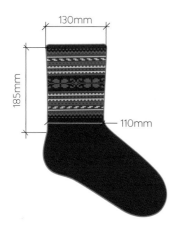

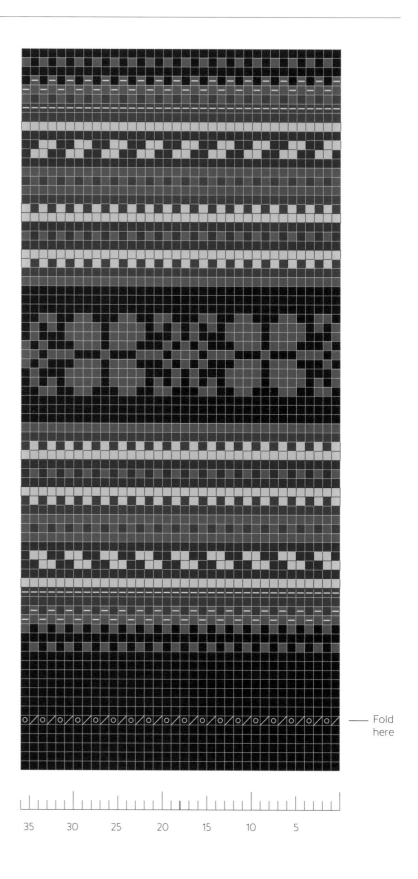

Fold here

WINTER FIELDS

Notes

Refer to Basic Sock Recipe for full instructions.

4 colours of yarn used: base colour (charcoal), and 3 contrast colours (light grey, dark grey and mid grey).

2–2.5mm needles and 2-ply wool.

1. Cast on 68 sts with base colour.

2. Divide equally between 4 needles on first round (17 sts per needle).

3. Work cuff following The Notches method (see Cuff Techniques).

4. Continue with leg, following chart pattern. Read chart from right to left and repeat twice.

5. With base colour, work 4 rounds straight.

6. Work heel with base colour, noting the variation in location of right and left heel flaps (see Basic Sock Recipe).

7. Work gusset with base colour.

8. Work foot with base colour.

9. Work toe with base colour, following Rounded Toe Cap and Finishing method (see Basic Sock Recipe).

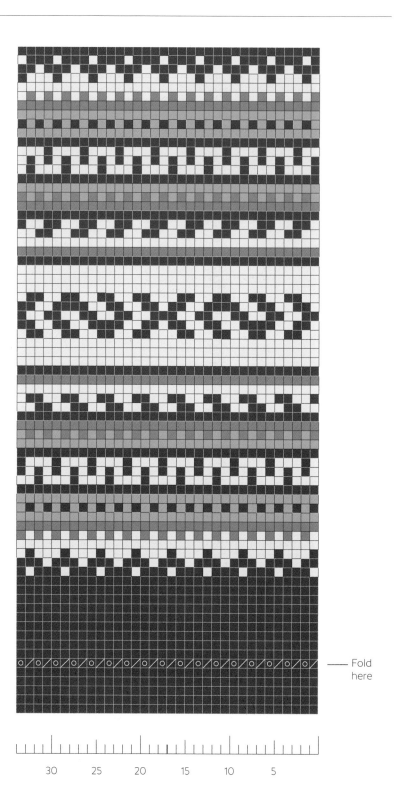

Fold here

30   25   20   15   10   5

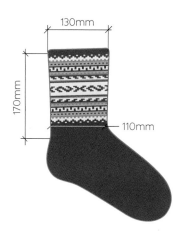

130mm

170mm

110mm

SUN SYMBOL

Notes

Refer to Basic Sock Recipe for full instructions.

5 colours of yarn used: base colour (charcoal), and 4 contrast colours (cream, red, green and yellow).

1.5–2mm needles and 2-ply wool.

1. Cast on 80 sts with base colour.

2. Divide equally between 4 needles on first round (20 sts per needle).

3. Work cuff following The Notches method (see Cuff Techniques).

4. Continue with leg, following chart pattern, increasing and decreasing where indicated to end with 72 sts. Read chart from right to left and repeat twice.

5. With base colour, work a further 8 rounds straight.

6. Work heel with base colour, noting the variation in location of right and left heel flaps (see Basic Sock Recipe).

7. Work gusset with base colour.

8. Work foot with base colour.

9. Work toe with base colour, following Banded Toe Cap and Finishing method (see Basic Sock Recipe).

Fold here

40 35 30 25 20 15 10 5

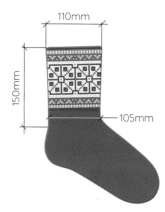

110mm

150mm

105mm

WINTER

Notes

Refer to Basic Sock Recipe for full instructions.

2 colours of yarn used: base colour (cream), and 1 contrast colour (black).

2–2.5mm needles and 2-ply wool.

1. Cast on 68 sts with base colour.

2. Divide equally between 4 needles on first round (17 sts per needle).

3. Work a (K2, P2) cuff for 15 rounds, as given in the chart.

4. Continue with leg, following chart pattern, increasing where indicated on chart, to create 70 sts for leg. Read each chart once from right to left, starting with right-hand chart.

5. Work heel with base colour over 34 sts, noting the variation in location of right and left heel flaps (see Basic Sock Recipe).

6. Maintaining chart pattern across all stitches, work gusset and foot.

7. Work toe with base colour, following Rounded Toe Cap and Finishing method (see Basic Sock Recipe).

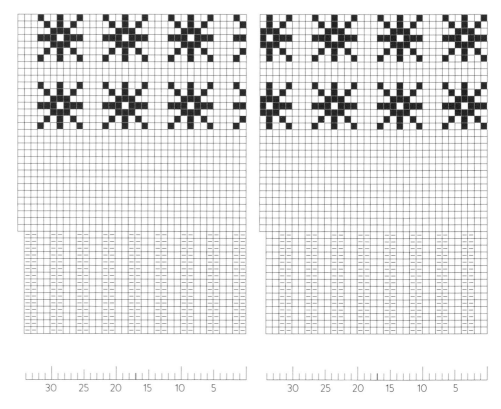

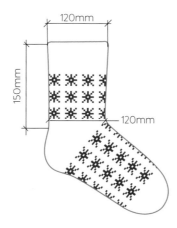

BLACK AND WHITE STAR

Notes

Refer to Basic Sock Recipe for full instructions.

2 colours of yarn used: base colour (white), and 1 contrast colour (black).

2–2.5mm needles and 4-ply yarn.

1. Cast on 72 sts with base colour.

2. Divide equally between 4 needles on first round (18 sts per needle).

3. Work 10 rounds of (K1, P1) rib following chart pattern, then continue with cuff and leg. Read chart from right to left and repeat twice.

4. On first half of the stitches, work heel following chart pattern, noting the shaping.

5. Continue with foot, maintaining pattern, ensuring that there is only a single row of white stitches at the centre of the Aureklis.

6. Work toe following chart pattern, noting the shaping. Repeat the chart twice for each round. If your foot length does not provide you with an easy pattern repeat for the toe, work in base colour.

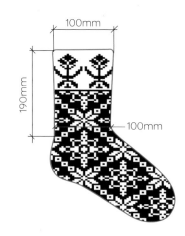

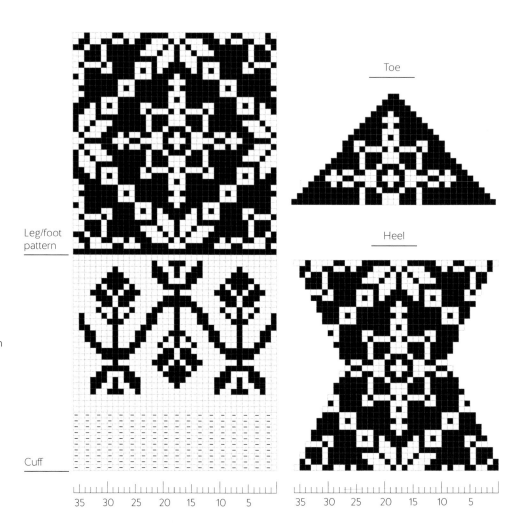

(Designed with reference to museum exhibit no: LM 43269:2, Kurzeme)

PINK LACE

Notes

Refer to Basic Sock Recipe for full instructions.

5 colours of yarn used: base colour (cream), and 4 contrast colours (deep purple, beige, pink and lilac).

2-2.5mm needles and 2-ply wool.

1. Cast on 64 sts with deep purple.

2. Divide equally between 4 needles on first round (16 sts per needle).

3. Work cuff and leg following colour chart pattern, decreasing where indicated on chart to finish with 60 sts after colour chart is complete. Read chart from right to left and repeat twice.

4. Continue with leg, working 16 rounds in total of 8-round lace pattern.

5. Work heel with base colour, noting the variation in location of right and left heel flaps (see Basic Sock Recipe).

6. Maintaining lace pattern over top half of stitches and working stocking stitch over bottom (heel) half of stitches, work gusset and foot.

7. Work toe with base colour, following Rounded Toe Cap and Finishing method (see Basic Sock Recipe).

Leg

Cuff

30   25   20   15   10   5

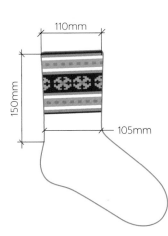

110mm

150mm

105mm

GREEN LACE

Notes

Refer to Basic Sock Recipe for full instructions.

4 colours of yarn used: base colour (cream), and 3 contrast colours (red, green and purple).

2–2.5mm needles and 2-ply wool.

1. Cast on 64 sts with base colour.

2. Divide equally between 4 needles on first round (16 sts per needle).

3. Work leg cuff and leg following colour chart pattern. Read chart from right to left and repeat twice.

4. Continue with leg, working 21 rounds in total of 7-row lace pattern.

5. Work heel with base colour, noting the variation in location of right and left heel flaps (see Basic Sock Recipe).

6. Maintaining lace pattern over top half of stitches and working stocking stitch over bottom (heel) half of stitches, work gusset and foot.

7. Work toe with base colour, following Rounded Toe Cap and Finishing method (see Basic Sock Recipe).

Leg

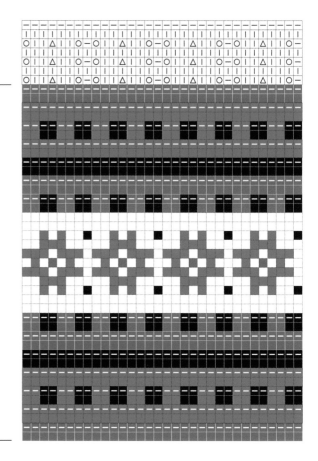

Cuff

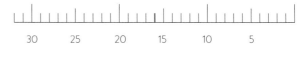

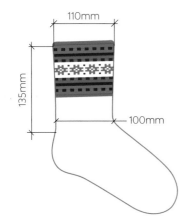

BLUE LACE

Notes

Refer to Basic Sock Recipe for full instructions.

5 colours of yarn used: base colour (cream), and 4 contrast colours (pale blue, dark blue, red and yellow).

2–2.5mm needles and 2-ply wool.

1. Cast on 64 sts with base colour.

2. Divide equally between 4 needles on first round (16 sts per needle).

3. Work cuff and leg following colour chart pattern. Read chart from right to left and repeat twice.

4. Continue with leg, working 16 rounds of 2-row lace pattern in total.

5. Work heel with base colour, noting the variation in location of right and left heel flaps (see Basic Sock Recipe).

6. Maintaining lace pattern over top half of stitches and working stocking stitch over bottom (heel) half of stitches, work gusset and foot.

7. Work toe with base colour, following Rounded Toe Cap and Finishing method (see Basic Sock Recipe).

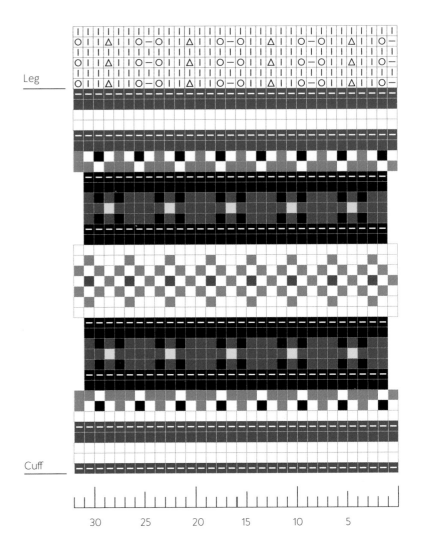

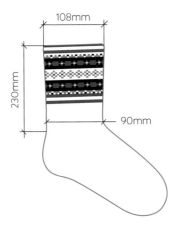

TURQUOISE

Notes

Refer to Basic Sock Recipe for full instructions.

6 colours of yarn used: base colour 4-ply (pale grey), and 5 contrast colours 2-ply (cream, mid-blue, deep blue, red and yellow).

2.5–3.5mm needles, 2-ply wool and 4-ply sock yarn.

1. Cast on 84 sts with cream 2-ply.

2. Divide equally between 4 needles on first round (21 sts per needle).

3. Work cuff and leg following colour chart pattern. Read chart from right to left and repeat twice, increasing and decreasing where indicated on chart, to finish with 72 sts for lace section, in base colour 4-ply.

4. Continue with lace section, working 20 rounds of 4-row lace pattern in total.

5. Work heel with base colour, noting the variation in location of right and left heel flaps (see Basic Sock Recipe).

6. Maintaining lace chart pattern over top half of stitches and working stocking stitch over bottom (heel) half of stitches, work gusset and foot.

7. Work toe with base colour, following Banded Toe Cap and Finishing method (see Basic Sock Recipe).

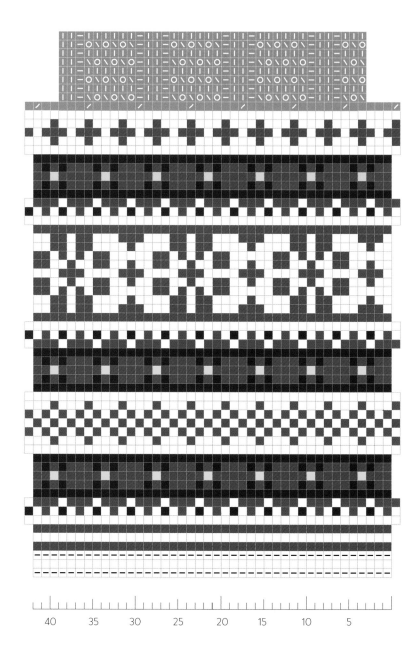

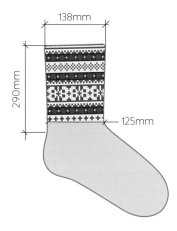

BALTIC WAVE

Notes

Refer to Basic Sock Recipe for full instructions.

2 colours of yarn used: base colour (cream), and 1 contrast colour (blue).

3–3.5mm needles and 6-ply sock yarn.

1. Cast on 60 sts with base colour.

2. Divide equally between 4 needles on first round (15 sts per needle).

3. Work cuff as given in the chart, purling the first round, knitting the second round and increasing on the third round to achieve 16 sts per needle.

4. Continue with leg, following chart pattern. Read chart from right to left and repeat 4 times.

5. Work heel with base colour, noting the variation in location of right and left heel flaps (see Basic Sock Recipe).

6. Maintaining chart pattern over top half of stitches and working stocking stitch over bottom (heel) half of stitches, work gusset and foot.

7. Work toe following Banded Toe Cap and Finishing method (see Basic Sock Recipe), maintaining chevron pattern over top half of stitches and working stocking stitch stripes over bottom half of stitches.

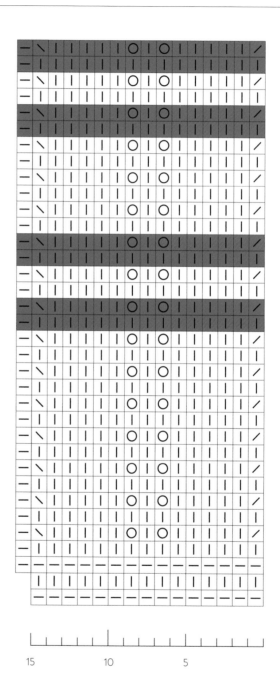

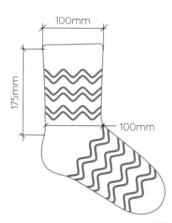

WARM GREY

Notes

Refer to Basic Sock Recipe for full instructions.

Single colour of yarn used: base colour (grey).

3–3.5mm needles and 6-ply sock yarn.

1. Cast on 60 sts with base colour.

2. Divide equally between 4 needles on first round (15 sts per needle).

3. Beginning with P2, work 15 rounds in (K2, P2) rib as given in the chart then continue with lace pattern. Read chart from right to left and repeat twice, working 40 rows of 10-row lace pattern in total.

4. Work heel with base colour, noting the variation in location of right and left heel flaps (see Basic Sock Recipe).

5. Maintaining lace pattern over top half of stitches and working stocking stitch over bottom (heel) half of stitches to end of toe, work gusset, foot and Banded Toe Cap and Finishing method (see Basic Sock Recipe).

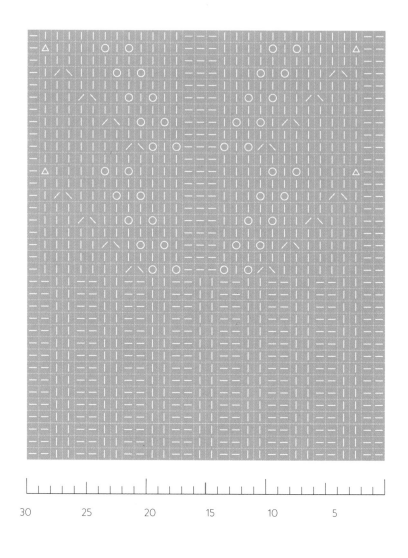

30   25   20   15   10   5

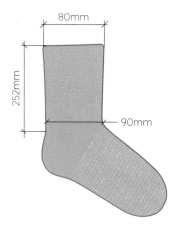

CHARCOAL

Notes

Refer to Basic Sock Recipe for full instructions.

Single colour of yarn used: base colour (charcoal).

3–3.5mm needles and 6-ply sock yarn.

1. Cast on 60 sts with base colour.

2. Divide equally between 4 needles on first round (15 sts per needle).

3. Work cuff following The Notches method (see Cuff Techniques).

4. Continue with leg, following chart lace pattern. Read chart from right to left and repeat chart twice, working 50 rounds of lace pattern in total.

5. Work heel with base colour, noting the variation in location of right and left heel flaps (see Basic Sock Recipe).

6. Maintaining lace pattern over top half of stitches and working stocking stitch over bottom (heel) half of stitches to end of toe, work gusset, foot and Banded Toe Cap and Finishing method (see Basic Sock Recipe).

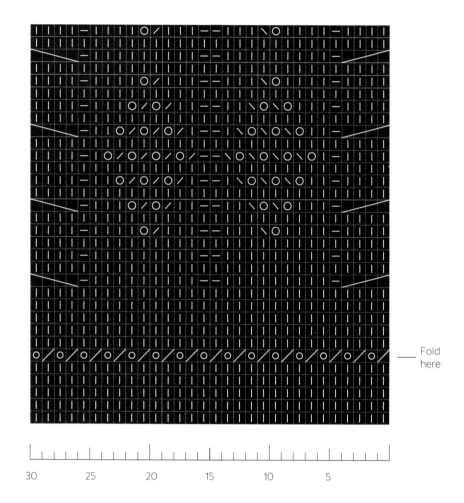

Fold here

30   25   20   15   10   5

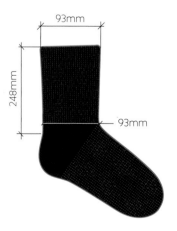

93mm

248mm

93mm

FIREWORK

Notes

Refer to Basic Sock Recipe for full instructions.

5 colours of yarn used: base colour (grey), and 4 contrast colours (red, charcoal, orange and cream).

2–2.5mm needles and 2-ply wool.

1. Cast on 72 sts with base colour.

2. Divide equally between 4 needles on first round (18 sts per needle).

3. Starting with a purl round, work Garter Stitch Cuff method (see Cuff Techniques) for the first 5 rounds, as given in the chart.

4. Continue with leg, following chart patterns and decreasing and increasing where indicated. Read each chart once from right to left, starting with right-hand chart.

5. Work heel with base colour, noting the variation in location of right and left heel flaps (see Basic Sock Recipe).

6. Work instep with base colour.

7. Work foot with base colour.

8. Work toe with base colour, following Banded Toe Cap and Finishing method (see Basic Sock Recipe).

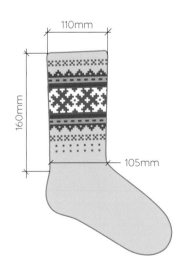

KURZEME

Notes

Refer to Basic Sock Recipe for full instructions.

4 colours of yarn used: base colour (white), and 3 contrast colours (black, orange and red).

2–2.5mm needles and 2-ply wool.

1. Cast on 76 sts with base colour.

2. Divide equally between 4 needles on first round (19 sts per needle).

3. Purl 1 round, then follow the chart, working a Latvian braid where indicated (see Cuff Techniques).

4. Continue with leg, following chart pattern. Read chart from right to left and repeat twice. Increase and decrease where indicated on chart to finish with 64 sts after chart is complete.

5. Continue in base colour for a further 18 rounds.

6. Work heel with base colour, noting the variation in location of right and left heel flaps (see Basic Sock Recipe).

7. Work instep with base colour.

8. Work foot with base colour.

9. Work toe with base colour, following Rounded Toe Cap and Finishing method (see Basic Sock Recipe).

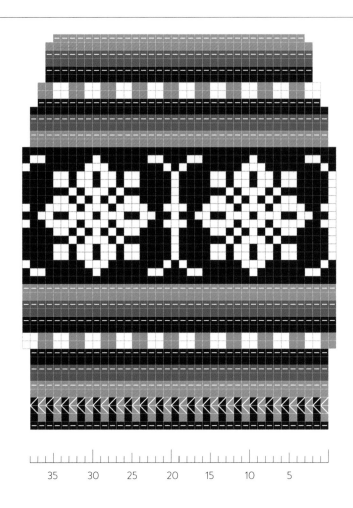

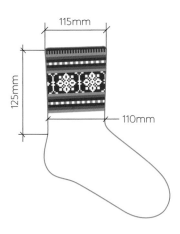

MORNING SUN

Notes

Refer to Basic Sock Recipe for full instructions.

4 colours of yarn used: base colour (cream), and 3 contrast colours (green, black and yellow).

2–2.5mm needles and 2-ply wool.

1. Cast on 72 sts with base colour.

2. Divide equally between 4 needles on first round (18 sts per needle).

3. Work cuff following The Notches method (see Cuff Techniques).

4. Continue with leg, following chart pattern. Read each chart once from right to left starting with the right-hand chart.

5. Continue in base colour for a further 10 rounds.

6. Work heel with base colour, noting the variation in location of right and left heel flaps (see Basic Sock Recipe).

7. Work instep with base colour.

8. Work foot with base colour.

9. Work toe with base colour, following Banded Toe Cap and Finishing method (see Basic Sock Recipe).

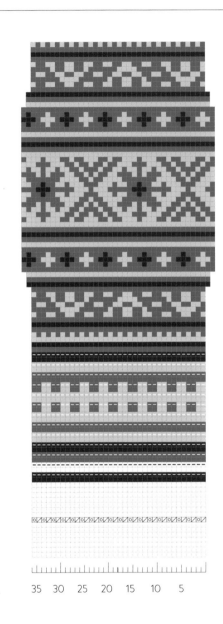

Fold here

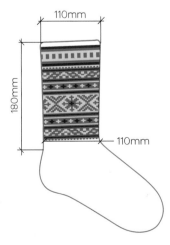

STARRY NIGHT

Notes

Refer to Basic Sock Recipe for full instructions.

3 colours of yarn used: base colour (black), and 2 contrast colours (dark grey and pale grey).

2–2.5mm needles and 2-ply wool.

1. Cast on 88 sts with pale grey.

2. Divide equally between 4 needles on first round (22 sts per needle).

3. Purl 1 round as given on chart, then follow chart pattern, working Latvian braid where indicated (see Cuff Techniques). Read chart from right to left and repeat twice, decreasing where indicated on chart to finish with 68 sts after chart is complete.

4. Continue in base colour for a further 5 rounds.

5. Decrease 4 sts evenly on the next round by working (k2tog, knit 15 sts) 4 times, to finish with 64 sts.

6. Continue in base colour for a further 12 rounds.

7. Work heel with base colour, noting the variation in location of right and left heel flaps (see Basic Sock Recipe).

8. Work instep with base colour.

9. Work foot with base colour.

10. Work toe with base colour, following Rounded Toe Cap and Finishing method (see Basic Sock Recipe).

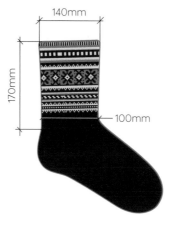

WEEKEND

Notes

Refer to Basic Sock Recipe for full instructions.

4 colours of yarn used: base colour (navy), and 3 contrast colours (orange, pink and cream).

1.5–2mm needles and 2-ply wool.

1. Cast on 80 sts with cream.

2. Divide equally between 4 needles on first round (20 sts per needle).

3. Work cuff following The Notches method (see Cuff Techniques).

4. Continue with leg, following chart pattern. Read chart from right to left and repeat twice. Increase and decrease where indicated on chart to finish with 80 sts after chart is complete.

5. Continue in base colour for a further 5 rounds.

6. Decrease 8 sts evenly on the next round by working (k2tog, knit 8 sts) 8 times, to finish with 72 sts.

7. Continue in base colour for a further 5 rounds.

8. Decrease 8 sts evenly on the next round by working (k2tog, knit 7 sts) 8 times to finish with 64 sts.

9. Work heel with base colour, noting the variation in location of right and left heel flaps (see Basic Sock Recipe).

10. Work instep with base colour.

11. Work foot with base colour.

12. Work toe with base colour, following Rounded Toe Cap and Finishing method (see Basic Sock Recipe).

— Fold here

40   35   30   25   20   15   10   5

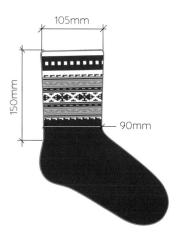

105mm

150mm

90mm

SERPENT

Notes

Refer to Basic Sock Recipe for full instructions.

5 colours of yarn used: base colour (cream), and 4 contrast colours (green, yellow, red and dark grey).

2–2.5mm needles and 2-ply wool.

1. Cast on 72 sts with base colour.

2. Divide equally between 4 needles on first round (18 sts per needle).

3. Purl 1 round, then knit 3 Latvian braids over the next 9 rounds (see Cuff Techniques).

4. Continue with leg, following chart pattern. Read chart from right to left and repeat twice. Increase and decrease where indicated to finish with 72 sts after chart is complete.

5. Work heel with base colour, noting the variation in location of right and left heel flaps (see Basic Sock Recipe).

6. Work instep with base colour.

7. Work foot with base colour.

8. Work toe with base colour, following Rounded Toe Cap and Finishing method (see Basic Sock Recipe).

40   35   30   25   20   15   10   5

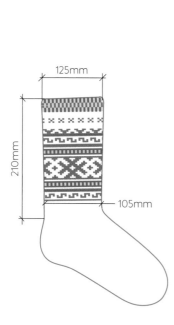

125mm

210mm

105mm

HOLIDAY

Notes

Refer to Basic Sock Recipe for full instructions.

3 colours of yarn used: base colour (navy blue), and 2 contrast colours (green and orange).

2–2.5mm needles and 2-ply wool.

1. Cast on 60 sts with base colour.

2. Divide between 4 needles on first round (15 sts per needle.

3. Continue with leg, following chart patterns. Read each chart once from right to left, starting with right-hand chart (see Techniques for Slipped Stitch).

4. Continue in base colour for a further 2 rounds.

5. Work heel with base colour, noting the variation in location of right and left heel flaps (see Basic Sock Recipe).

6. Work instep with base colour.

7. Work foot with base colour.

8. Work toe with base colour, following Banded Toe Cap and Finishing method (see Basic Sock Recipe).

| 30 | 25 | 20 | 15 | 10 | 5 |

| 30 | 25 | 20 | 15 | 10 | 5 |

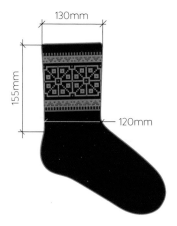

130mm

155mm

120mm

PINK NET

Notes

Refer to Basic Sock Recipe for full instructions.

5 colours of yarn used: base colour (marled grey), and 4 contrast colours (deep pink, blue, black and orange).

2.5–3mm needles and 2-ply wool.

1. Cast on 60 sts with base colour.

2. Divide between 4 needles on first round (15 sts per needle.

3. Continue with leg, following chart patterns. Read each chart once from right to left, starting with right-hand chart (see Techniques for Slipped Stitch).

4. Continue in base colour for a further 2 rounds.

5. Work heel with base colour, noting the variation in location of right and left heel flaps (see Basic Sock Recipe).

6. Work instep with base colour.

7. Work foot with base colour.

8. Work toe with base colour, following Banded Toe Cap and Finishing method (see Basic Sock Recipe).

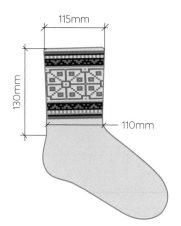

GOLDEN STRIPES

Notes

Refer to Basic Sock Recipe for full instructions.

4 colours of yarn used: base colour (cream), and 3 contrast colours (yellow, orange and black).

2–3mm needles and 2-ply wool.

1. Cast on 72 sts with orange.

2. Divide equally between 4 needles on first round (18 sts per needle).

3. Work leg following chart pattern. Read chart from right to left and repeat twice.

4. Work heel with base colour, noting the variation in location of right and left heel flaps (see Basic Sock Recipe).

5. Work gusset with base colour.

6. Work foot with base colour.

7. Work toe with base colour, following Banded Toe Cap and Finishing method (see Basic Sock Recipe).

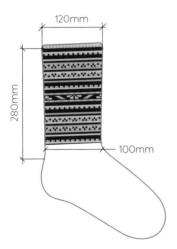

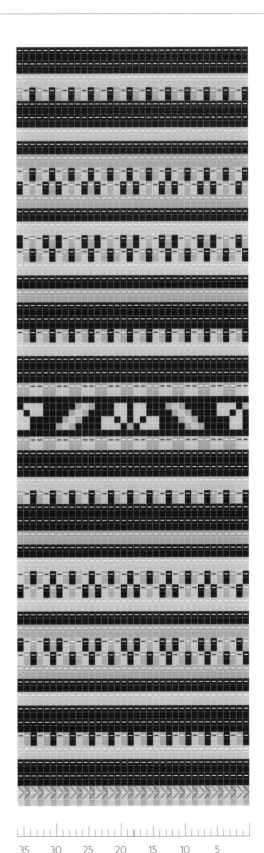

(Designed with reference to museum exhibit no: KNM 8134)

FESTIVE

Notes

Refer to Basic Sock Recipe for full instructions.

6 colours of yarn used: base colour (cream), and 5 contrast colours (blue, yellow, red, green and brown).

2–3mm needles and 2-ply wool.

1. Cast on 72 sts with base colour.

2. Divide equally between 4 needles on first round (18 sts per needle).

3. Work leg following chart pattern and working Latvian braids (see Cuff Techniques). Read chart from right to left and repeat twice.

4. With base colour, work 4 more rounds straight.

5. Work heel with base colour, noting the variation in location of right and left heel flaps (see Basic Sock Recipe).

6. Work foot with base colour.

7. Work toe with base colour, following Banded Toe Cap and Finishing method (see Basic Sock Recipe).

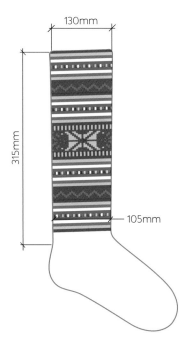

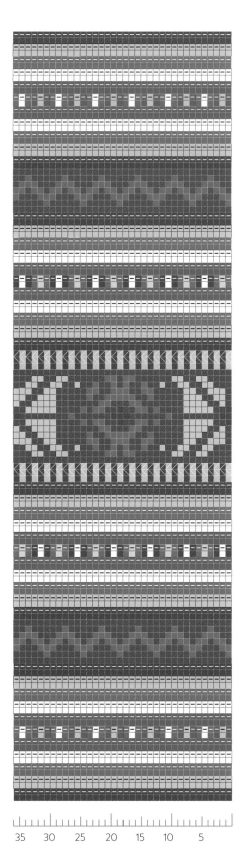

(Designed with reference to museum exhibit no: KNM 8144)

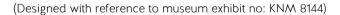

ORANGE STAR

Notes

Refer to Basic Sock Recipe for full instructions.

5 colours of yarn used: base colour (cream), and 4 contrast colours (orange, yellow, black and teal).

2–3mm needles and 2-ply wool.

1. Cast on 72 sts with orange.

2. Divide equally between 4 needles on first round (18 sts per needle).

3. Work leg following chart pattern, increasing and decreasing where indicated. Read chart from right to left and repeat twice.

4. With base colour, work 14 rounds straight.

5. Work heel with base colour, noting the variation in location of right and left heel flaps (see Basic Sock Recipe).

6. Work foot with base colour.

7. Work toe with base colour, following Banded Toe Cap and Finishing method (see Basic Sock Recipe).

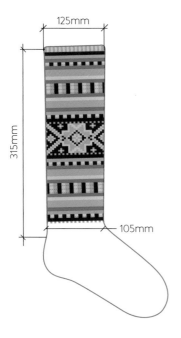

(Designed with reference to museum exhibit no: KNM 8135)

BRIGHT ANKLE

Notes

Refer to Basic Sock Recipe for full instructions.

4 colours of yarn used: base colour (black), and 3 contrast colours (orange, green and blue).

2–2.5mm needles and 4-ply sock yarn.

1. Cast on 80 sts with base colour.

2. Divide equally between 4 needles on first round (20 sts each needle).

3. Work 10 rounds of (P1, K1) rib following cuff chart pattern. Read chart from right to left and repeat twice.

4. Continue with leg in base colour and when sock measures 19cm from cast-on edge, decrease as follows: on next round, decrease at the end of the second and fourth needles (to decrease 2 sts). Knit 5 rounds. Repeat the last 6 rounds 3 times more to end with 72 sts.

5. Continue straight until sock measures 32cm from cast-on edge.

6. Work ankle pattern, following chart. Read chart from right to left and repeat twice.

7. Work gusset with base colour.

8. Work foot with base colour.

9. Work toe with base colour, following Rounded Toe Cap and Finishing method (see Basic Sock Recipe).

Ankle pattern

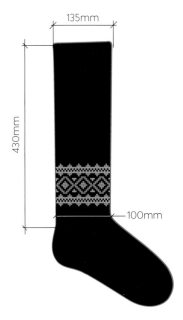

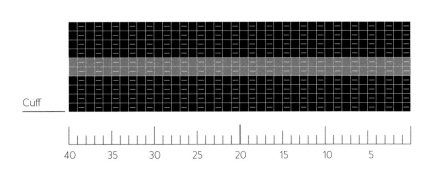

Cuff

(Designed with reference to museum exhibit no: MNM 2961:1-2, Piebalga. Early 19th century)

PATTERNED ANKLE

Notes

Refer to Basic Sock Recipe for full instructions.

2 colours of yarn used: base colour (cream), and 1 contrast colour (black).

2–2.5mm needles and 4-ply sock yarn.

1. Cast on 80 sts with base colour.

2. Divide equally between 4 needles on first round (20 sts each needle).

3. Work 12 rounds of (P1, K1) rib following cuff chart pattern. Read chart once from right to left and repeat twice.

4. Continue with leg in base colour and when sock measures 17cm from cast-on edge, decrease as follows: on next round, decrease 1 st at the end of the second and fourth needles (to decrease 2 sts). Knit 5 rounds. Repeat the last 6 rounds 3 times more to end with 72 sts.

5. Continue straight until sock measures 30cm from cast-on edge.

6. Work ankle pattern, following charts. Read each chart once from right to left, starting with right-hand chart.

7. With base colour, work 3 rounds straight.

8. Work heel, gusset and foot in base colour.

9. Work toe with base colour, following Rounded Toe Cap and Finishing method (see Basic Sock Recipe).

Leg pattern

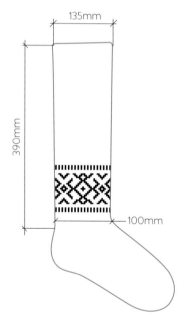

Cuff

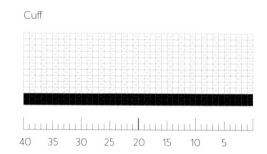

SUITI

Notes

Refer to Basic Sock Recipe for full instructions

3 colours of yarn used: base colour (cream), and 2 contrast colours (deep pink and navy blue).

1.5mm, 2mm and 2.5mm needles and 2-ply wool.

1. Cast on 96 sts with base colour and 2mm needles.

2. Divide equally between 4 needles on first round (24 sts per needle).

3. Work a (K1, P1) cuff for 10 rounds, as given in chart.

4. Continue with leg, following chart pattern. Read each chart once from right to left, starting with right-hand chart, using needles as follows: for first, third and fourth chart repeats use 2mm needles, for second chart repeat use 2.5mm needles, for remainder of sock use 1.5mm needles.

5. Work heel with base colour, noting the variation in location of right and left heel flaps (see Basic Sock Recipe).

6. Maintaining chart pattern, work gusset and foot.

7. Maintaining chart pattern, work toe following Banded Toe Cap and Finishing method (see Basic Sock Recipe).

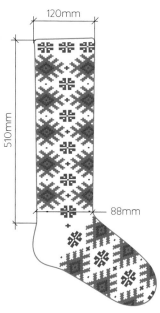

BLACK AND WHITE STAR

Notes

Refer to Basic Sock Recipe for full instructions.

2 colours of yarn used: base colour (white), and 1 contrast colour (black).

2–2.5mm needles and 4-ply sock yarn.

1. Cast on 78 sts with base colour.

2. Divide equally between 4 needles on first round (19 sts on 2 needles and 20 sts on two needles).

3. Work 7 rounds of chevron rib following chart pattern then continue with leg. Read chart from right to left and repeat twice. Work 8 full repeats of lace pattern for leg, then work 1 decrease round of (K2tog, K11) 6 times to finish with 72 sts.

4. Continue with ankle pattern following chart. Read each chart once from right to left, starting with right-hand chart.

5. Now follow instructions for the short version of Black and White Star socks, from Step 4 to the end.

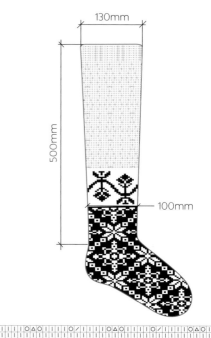

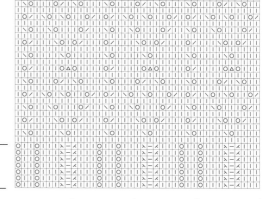

Leg

Cuff

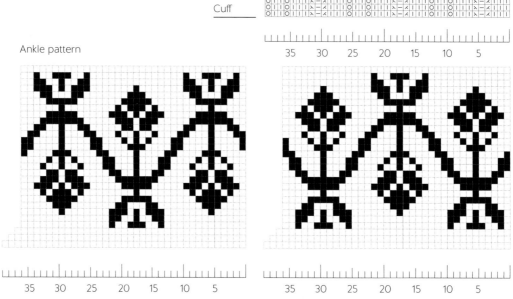

Ankle pattern

(Designed with reference to museum exhibit no: LM 43269:2, Kurzeme)

BLACK FLOWER

Notes

Refer to Basic Sock Recipe for full instructions.

2 colours of yarn used: base colour (cream), and 1 contrast colour (black).

2–2.5mm needles and 4-ply sock yarn.

1. Cast on 104 sts with base colour.

2. Divide equally between 4 needles on first round (26 sts each needle).

3. Work 13 rounds of chevron rib following chart pattern. Read chart from right to left and repeat twice.

4. Continue with leg. Work 92 rounds of lace pattern, decreasing where indicated on chart to end with 80 sts.

5. Continue with leg, following colour chart patterns. Read each chart from right to left, starting with right-hand chart.

6. On first half of the stitches, work heel following chart pattern, noting the shaping.

7. Maintaining pattern, continue with gusset and foot.

8. Maintaining pattern, work toe following Rounded Toe Cap and Finishing method (see Basic Sock Recipe).

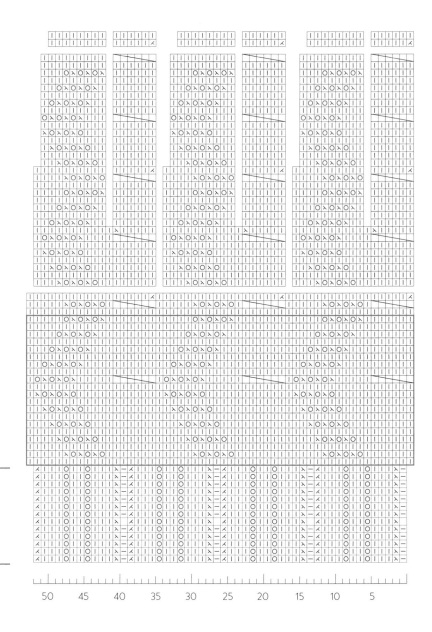

(Designed with reference to museum exhibit no: LM 42732:1, Kurzeme)

Heel

| 40 | 35 | 30 | 25 | 20 | 15 | 10 | 5 |

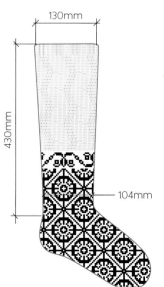

130mm

430mm

104mm

YELLOW LACE

Notes

Refer to Basic Sock Recipe for full instructions.

Single colour of yarn used: base colour (yellow).

2–2.5mm needles and 4-ply sock yarn.

1. Cast on 88 sts with base colour.

2. Divide equally between 4 needles on first round (22 sts each needle).

3. Work 10 rounds of rib following chart pattern. Read chart from right to left and repeat twice.

4. Continue with leg, following chart pattern, decreasing where indicated on chart to end with 72 sts.

5. Work Flat Heel with base colour (see Basic Sock Recipe).

6. Maintaining chart pattern across top half of stitches and working stocking stitch on bottom half of stitches, work gusset and foot.

7. Work toe following Banded Toe Cap and Finishing method (see Basic Sock Recipe).

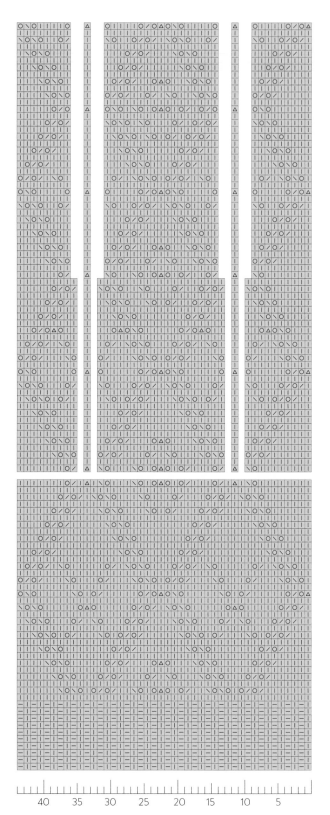

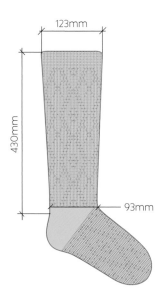

(Designed with reference to museum exhibit no: LM 30346:1, Kurzeme)

BLACK SUN

Notes

Refer to Basic Sock Recipe for full instructions.

2 colours of yarn used: base colour (cream) and 1 contrast colour (black).

2–2.5mm needles and 4-ply sock yarn.

1. With base colour, work as given for Yellow Lace Socks, until 3 full repeats of diamond lace pattern have been worked, ending with 80 sts.

2. Continue with leg, following colour chart patterns. Read each chart once from right to left, starting with right-hand chart.

3. Work Flat Heel (see Basic Sock Recipe) on first half of stitches, following chart and noting the shaping.

4. Maintaining chart pattern, work foot across all sts.

5. Maintaining chart pattern, work flat toe.

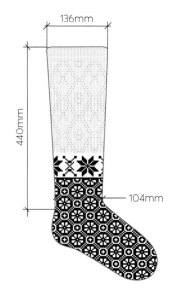

Heel

(Designed with reference to museum exhibit no: LM 30346:1, Kurzeme)

WHITE LACE

Notes

Refer to Basic Sock Recipe for full instructions.

Single colour of yarn used: base colour (white).

2–2.5mm needles and 4-ply sock yarn.

1. Cast on 96 sts with base colour and 2.5mm needles.

2. Divide equally between 4 needles on first round (24 sts each needle).

3. Work 10 rounds of (K1, P1) rib following chart pattern. Read chart from right to left and repeat twice.

4. Continue with leg, following chart pattern, decreasing where indicated on chart to end with 64 sts.

5. Work Flat Heel with base colour (see Basic Sock Recipe).

6. Maintaining chart pattern across top half of stitches and working stocking stitch on bottom half of stitches, work gusset and foot.

7. Work flat toe following chart, noting the decreases.

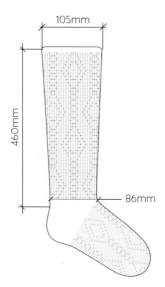

(Designed with reference to museum exhibit no: BDM Nr.27487, Barta. Early 19th century)

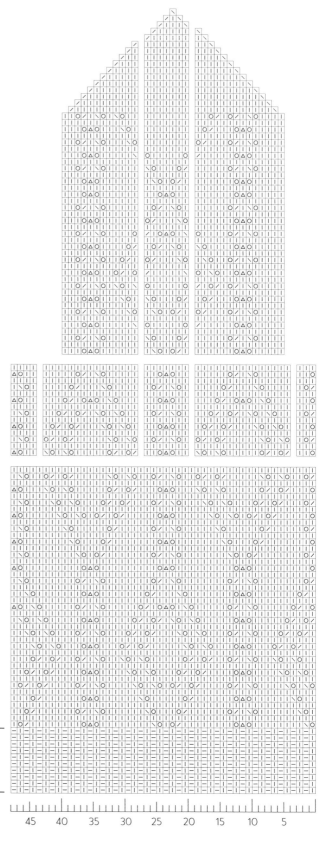

Leg

Cuff

45 40 35 30 25 20 15 10 5

PASTEL LACE

Notes

Refer to Basic Sock Recipe for full instructions.

Single colour of yarn used: base colour (pale pink).

2–2.5mm needles and 4-ply sock yarn.

1. Cast on 96 sts with base colour.

2. Divide equally between 4 needles on first round (24 sts each needle).

3. Work 10 rounds of (K1, P1) rib following chart pattern. Read chart from right to left and repeat twice.

4. Continue with leg, following chart pattern, decreasing where indicated on chart to end with 72 sts. Read chart from right to left and repeat twice and work 12.5 pattern repeats in total.

5. Work Flat Heel (see Basic Sock Recipe).

6. Maintaining chart pattern across top half of stitches and working stocking stitch on bottom half of stitches, work gusset and foot.

7. Work toe following Banded Toe Cap and Finishing method (see Basic Sock Recipe).

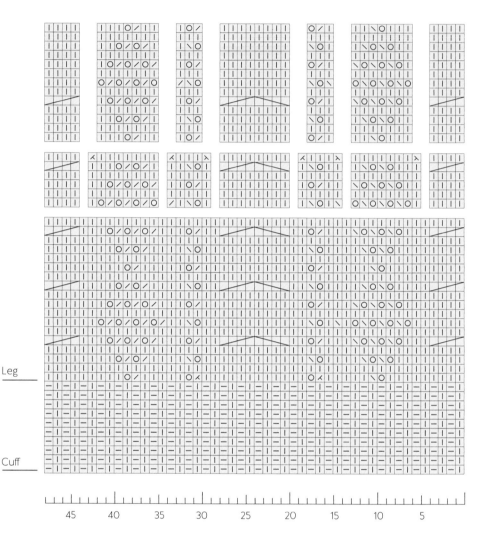

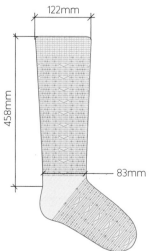

(Designed with reference to museum exhibit no: LM 43269:2, Kurzeme)

LONG LACE

Notes

Refer to Basic Sock Recipe for full instructions.

1 colour of yarn used: base colour (grey).

3–3.5mm needles and 6-ply sock yarn.

1. Cast on 64 sts with base colour.

2. Divide equally between 4 needles on first round (16 sts per needle).

3. Work cuff following The Notches method (see Cuff Techniques).

4. Continue with leg, following chart pattern. Read chart from right to left and repeat the chart stitches 4 times for each round. Work the 18 rounds of the pattern a total of 6 times, while decreasing at the beginning of the third and fifth repeats as follows:

- decrease 1 st at the beginning of the third repeat by working p2tog, P1 at beginning of round (instead of P3), and on subsequent rounds purl the first 2 sts.

- decrease 1 st at the beginning of the fifth repeat by working p2tog at the beginning of round, and on subsequent rounds purl the first stitch.

After working 6 repeats of the chart rows, you will end the leg with 56 sts.

5. Work heel, noting the variation in location of right and left heel flaps (see Basic Sock Recipe).

6. Maintaining chart pattern across top half of stitches and working stocking stitch on bottom half of stitches, work gusset and foot.

7. Work toe following Banded Toe Cap and Finishing method (see Basic Sock Recipe).

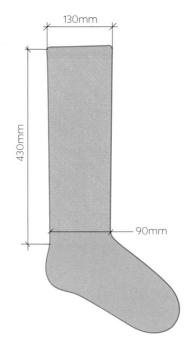

130mm

430mm

90mm

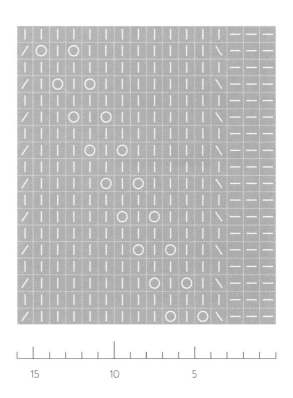

15   10   5

LONG LEAF

Notes

Refer to Basic Sock Recipe for full instructions.

1 colour of yarn used: base colour (cream).

3–3.5mm needles and 6-ply sock yarn.

1. Cast on 64 sts with base colour.

2. Divide equally between 4 needles on first round (16 sts per needle).

3. Work cuff following The Notches method (see Cuff Techniques).

4. Continue with leg, following chart pattern. Read chart from right to left and repeat chart stitches 4 times for each round. Work the 16 rounds of the chart pattern a total of 6 times, whilst decreasing as follows:

- decrease 1 st at the beginning of the fourth pattern repeat by working p2tog at beginning of each chart repeat (instead of P2), and incorporate decreased stitches into the subsequent rounds.

After working 6 repeats of the pattern rows, you will end the leg with 60 sts.

5. Work heel, noting the variation in location of right and left heel flaps (see Basic Sock Recipe).

6. Maintaining chart pattern across top half of stitches and working stocking stitch on bottom half of stitches, work gusset and foot.

7. Work toe following Rounded Toe Cap and Finishing method (see Basic Sock Recipe).

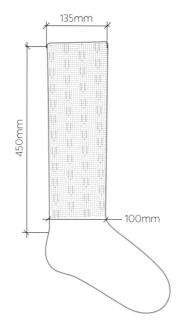

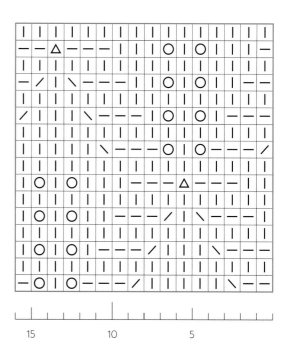

SUITI ZIG ZAG

Notes

Refer to Basic Sock Recipe for full instructions.

4 colours of yarn used: base colour (navy blue) and 3 contrast colours (bright pink, green and yellow).

2–2.5mm needles and 4-ply sock yarn.

1. Cast on 96 sts with base colour.

2. Divide equally between 4 needles on first round (24 sts each needle).

3. Work 10 rounds of (K1, P1) rib following chart pattern. Read chart from right to left and repeat 4 times.

4. Continue with leg, following chart pattern, decreasing where indicated on chart to end with 72 sts. Read chart from right to left and repeat twice and work a total of 13 5-row stripes.

5. Work heel with base colour (see Basic Sock Recipe).

6. Maintaining chart pattern across top half of stitches and working stocking stitch on bottom half of stitches, work gusset and foot.

7. Work toe with base colour, following Banded Toe Cap and Finishing method (see Basic Sock Recipe).

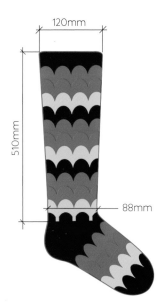

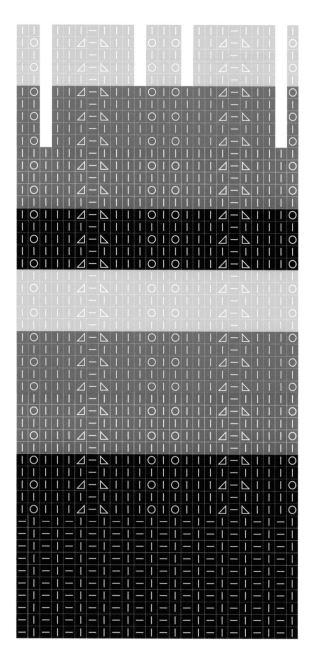

COLOURFUL

Notes

Refer to Basic Sock Recipe for full instructions.

6 colours of yarn used: base colour (black), and 5 contrast colours (purple, bright pink, red, yellow and bright green).

2–3mm needles and 2-ply wool.

1. Cast on 96 sts with base colour.

2. Divide equally between 4 needles on first round (24 sts per needle).

3. Work cuff following The Notches method (see Cuff Techniques)

4. Continue with leg, following chart patterns, decreasing where indicated, to end with 72 sts. Read each chart once from right to left, starting with right-hand chart.

5. Work heel with base colour, noting the variation in location of right and left heel flaps (see Basic Sock Recipe).

6. Work gusset and top of foot with main chart, beginning base of foot after completing heel from separate chart.

7. Work toe with base colour, following Rounded Toe Cap and Finishing method (see Basic Sock Recipe).

8. Make an i-cord in contrast yarn that is long enough to tie around leg and thread through eyelets (see Techniques).

45 40 35 30 25 20 15 10 5   45 40 35 30 25 20 15 10 5

Fold here

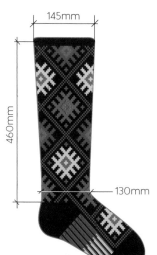

145mm

460mm

130mm

Base of foot

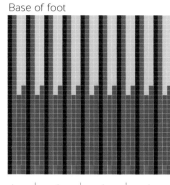

35 30 25 20 15 10 5

DAGDA

Notes

5 colours of yarn used: base colour (grey), and 4 contrast colours (white, pale grey, black and red).

2–3mm needles and 6-ply sock yarn.

1. Cast on 64 sts with base colour.

2. Divide equally between 4 needles on first round (16 sts per needle).

3. Work cuff following The Notches method (see Cuff Techniques).

4. Continue with main section, following chart pattern. Read chart from right to left and repeat twice, ending with The Notches method as indicated.

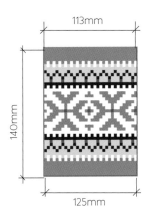

Fold here

BALVI

Notes

7 colours of yarn used: base colour (burgundy), and 6 contrast colours (red, yellow, cream, brown, pale green and dark green).

2–2.5mm needles and 2-ply wool.

1. Cast on 80 sts with base colour.

2. Divide equally between 4 needles on first round (20 sts per needle).

3. Work cuff following chart pattern. Read chart from right to left and repeat twice.

4. Continue with main section, following chart pattern and decreasing where indicated to finish with 72 sts. Read chart from right to left and repeat twice.

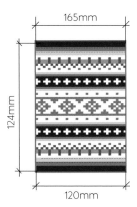

LACE

Notes

1 colour of yarn used throughout: base colour (grey).

2–3mm needles and 6-ply sock yarn.

1. Cast on 56 sts.

2. Divide equally between 4 needles on first round (14 sts per needle).

3. Purl first 2 rounds, then follow chart pattern. Read chart from right to left and repeat 4 times. Work a total of 10 8-row chart repeats.

4. Purl 2 rounds, then cast off.

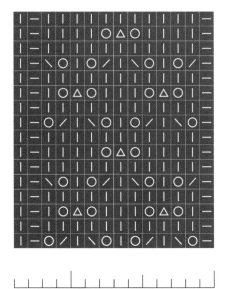

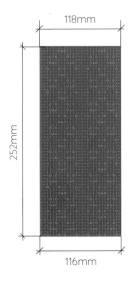

GREY-RED ZIG ZAG

Notes

3 colours of yarn used: base colour (grey), and 2 contrast colours (red and black).

2–3.5mm needles and 6-ply sock yarn.

1. Cast on 72 sts with base colour and larger needles.

2. Divide equally between 4 needles on first round (18 sts per needle).

3. Following chart, work a (K2, P2) cuff for 10 rounds.

4. Continue with main leg, following chart pattern. Read chart from right to left and repeat twice, changing to smaller needles after completing the first full pattern repeat.

5. After working 2.5 full pattern repeats, end with 16 rounds of (K2, P2) rib.

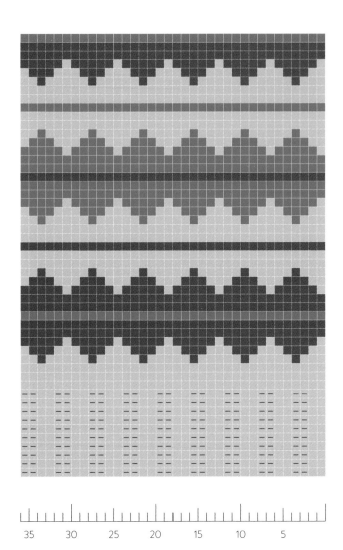

35 30 25 20 15 10 5

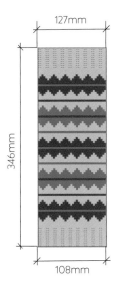

127mm

346mm

108mm

PINK ZIG ZAG

Notes

2 colours of yarn used: base colour (black), and 1 contrast colour (bright pink).

2–2.5mm needles and 2-ply sock yarn.

1. Cast on 96 sts with base colour and larger needles.

2. Divide equally between 4 needles on first round (24 sts per needle).

3. Following chart, work a (K2, P2) cuff for 24 rounds.

4. Continue with main leg, following chart pattern. Read chart from right to left and repeat twice, changing to smaller needles after completing the first 7 pattern repeats.

5. After working 14 full pattern repeats, end with 18 rounds of (K2, P2) rib.

(Designed with reference to museum exhibit no: MNM Nr.1933, Audona. Early 19th century)

BRIGHT STARS

Notes

4 colours of yarn used: base colour (purple), and 3 contrast colours (blue, red and yellow).

2–3mm needles and 2-ply wool.

1. Cast on 108 sts with base colour.

2. Divide equally between 4 needles on first round (27 sts per needle).

3. Following chart, work a (K2, P2) cuff for 10 rounds.

4. Continue with leg, following chart pattern, increasing where indicated to work on 116 sts. Read chart from right to left and repeat twice, changing to smaller needles after completing the first 2 full pattern repeats

5. After working 4 full pattern repeats, end with 10 rounds of (K2, P2) rib.

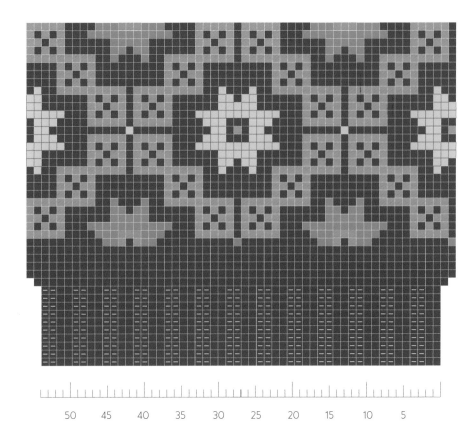

50	45	40	35	30	25	20	15	10	5	

153mm

396mm

137mm

NAVY GRID

Notes

4 colours of yarn used: base colour (pale grey), and 3 contrast colours (navy blue, bright green and bright pink).

2–2.5mm needles and 2-ply wool.

1. Cast on 96 sts with base colour.

2. Divide equally between 4 needles on first round (24 sts per needle).

3. Following chart, work a (K2, P2) cuff for 10 rounds.

4. Continue with leg, following chart pattern, decreasing where indicated. Starting with right-hand chart, read each chart once from right to left, ending with 10 rounds of (K2, P2) rib.

45 40 35 30 25 20 15 10 5

45 40 35 30 25 20 15 10 5

STAR

Notes

4 colours of yarn used: base colour (burgundy), and 3 contrast colours (blue, turquoise and white).

2–2.5mm needles and 2-ply sock yarn.

1. Cast on 96 sts with base colour.

2. Divide equally between 4 needles on first round (24 sts per needle).

3. Following chart, work a (K1, P1) rib for 10 rounds.

4. Continue with leg, following chart pattern, decreasing where indicated. Read chart from right to left, ending with 10 rounds of (K1, P1) rib.

5. For stirrups, cast on 48 sts with base colour and knit 22 rows of garter stitch (every row knit). Cast off and sew row-ends to inner ankle edge, in line with start of rib.

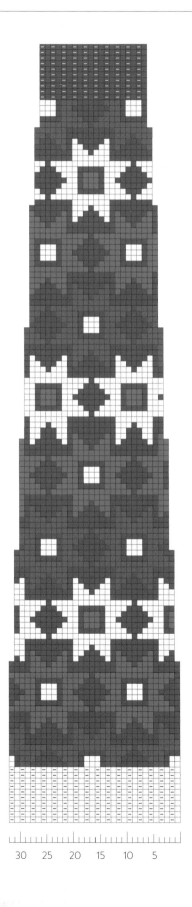

30 25 20 15 10 5

Techniques

KNITTING SYMBOLS

This handy guide explains the symbols used in the charts and the mitten knitting pattern (see Knitting Socks):

INSTRUCTIONS	SYMBOL IN CHART	SYMBOL IN SOCK RECIPE
Knit stitch (K) – Insert the right needle into the front of the next stitch on left needle, wrap the yarn around the right needle from back to front and pull the needle through the stitch to the front of work to create a loop on right needle. Take the original stitch off the tip of the left needle, leaving the new knit stitch on the right needle. The knit stitch is represented on a chart by a blank square.	□ |	
Purl stitch (P) – Insert the right needle into the next stitch on the left needle from the back of the stitch to the front, wrap the yarn around the right needle anti-clockwise and pull the needle through the stitch to the back of work to create a loop on right needle. Take the original stitch off the tip of the left needle, leaving the new purl stitch on the right needle.	—	
K2tog (knit 2 stitches together) – Insert the right needle into the next 2 stitches on left needle and knit them together as one stitch. The left stitch wraps over the right stitch, which creates a decrease of 1 stitch, slanting to the right.	◢ ◸	◸
SKPO (slip, knit, pass over) – Insert the right needle into the next stitch knitwise and slip the stitch to the right needle, without knitting it. Knit the next stitch. Insert the left needle into the slipped stitch on the right needle. Lift the slipped stitch and pass it over the knitted stitch and off the needle. The right stitch wraps over the left stitch and creates a decrease of 1 stitch, slanting to the left.	◥ ◿	◺
P2tog (purl 2 stitches together) – Insert the right needle (as if to purl) into the next 2 stitches on left needle and purl them together as one stitch.		◿
Double left-slanting decrease – Insert the right needle into the next stitch knitwise and slip the stitch to the right needle, without knitting it. Knit the next 2 stitches together as one stitch. Insert the left needle into the slipped stitch on the right needle. Lift the slipped stitch and pass it over the k2tog stitches and off the needle. This creates a decrease of 2 stitches, slanting to the left.	△	△

INSTRUCTIONS	SYMBOL IN CHART
Slipped stitch – This creates a two-coloured pattern because the stitch that you slip is still in the colour of yarn from the previous row, whereas the stitch that you knit is in the current colour of yarn. For example, on the first of the two rows, you would purl a stitch (in White), and knit a stitch (in Red), then on the next round, you knit the stitch in White and slip the Red stitch.	
C4F (cable front over 4 stitches) – slip next 2 sts onto a cable needle, hold at front of work, knit next 2 sts then knit 2 sts from cable needle (for a left slanting cable).	
C4B (cable back over 4 stitches) – slip next 2 sts onto a cable needle, hold at back of work, knit next 2 sts then knit 2 sts from cable needle (for a right slanting cable).	
Yarn over – Wrap the yarn over the needle to add an extra stitch.	

BASIC SOCK RECIPE

GETTING STARTED

All of the socks in this book follow the same basic knitting pattern, which consists of a cuff, leg, heel, instep, foot and toe.

To make your socks, follow the instructions opposite (see Knitting Socks), alongside the colour chart of your chosen design, to create your Latvian socks.

The sock recipe and charts use symbols that are fully explained in the Knitting Symbols table. It is important to first familiarise yourself with the symbols used.

Remember to check your tension before knitting a full sock, as the basic knitting pattern is based on achieving the correct tension (see How to Use this Book).

Note that with the correct tension, the socks will fit different ankle circumferences, depending on the number of ankle stitches within the pattern, as follows:

Ankle stitches	56	60	64	68	72
Ankle circumference	18.75cm (7½in)	20cm (8in)	21.5cm (8½in)	22.75cm (9in)	24cm (9½in)

You can also adapt most socks to fit your own ankle circumference if desired, and this is explained in the Leg section (see Knitting Socks: Step 3)

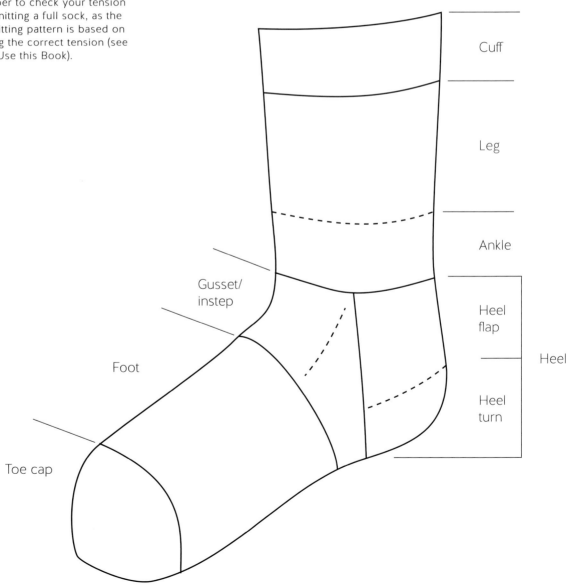

Cuff

Leg

Ankle

Heel flap

Heel

Heel turn

Gusset/ instep

Foot

Toe cap

KNITTING SOCKS

STEP 1 – CASTING ON

1. Using any cast-on method, cast on the total amount of stitches onto one needle, making sure you leave a long tail end of yarn. The total amount of stitches you need is specified in each pattern; note that some socks have a wider or looser cuff than others, depending on the style.

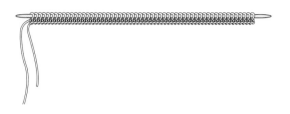

2. Divide the stitches equally over 4 double pointed needles when working the first round of the cuff. Each pattern will tell you how many stitches to place onto each needle.

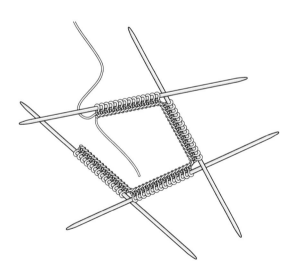

3. Tie the cast-on tail end with the working yarn, so that there is no gap between the stitches on the first and last needles.

4. Use one of the yarn tails as a marker to indicate the start of the round.

5. Always knit from right to left.

STEP 2 – THE CUFF

Start the cuff according to the pattern (see Cuff Techniques for instructions for The Notches and Latvian Braid).

The cuff is usually knitted to a depth of 15cm (6in), or according to the chosen design.

You can customise your cuff by making it longer or shorter than specified. If you find the notches cuff too advanced, you can substitute with a simple Knit-Purl cuff as follows: after casting on, purl the first round, knit the second round, purl the third round and knit the fourth round. Then start knititng according to the pattern.

STEP 3 – THE LEG

The rest of the leg is completed in either stocking stitch (knitting every round) or garter stitch, following the pattern and reading the chart from right to left on every round. Where only 1 chart is provided, this chart is repeated twice. Where 2 charts are provided, each chart is knitted once.

For some patterns, there are additional rounds to knit after the chart is completed, and you may need to decrease to reach the correct number of stitches for the ankle, heel and foot.

Each pattern will specify how to decrease and at this point you can adjust the pattern to fit your ankle. For example, if you have 72 stitches for your cuff, you may wish to work additional decrease rounds, to achieve less stitches for a smaller ankle circumference (see Getting Started).

STEP 4

PART A – THE HEEL FLAP (FOR RIGHT FOOT)

1. When the leg is completed, and the final round has been worked, slide all of the stitches from Needle 2 onto Needle 1.

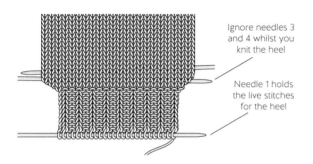

Ignore needles 3 and 4 whilst you knit the heel

Needle 1 holds the live stitches for the heel

These are now the heel stitches and they account for half of your total sock stitches.

The number of heel stitches now on Needle 1 for each size, are listed below:

Sock stitches	56	60	64	68	72
Heel stitches	28	30	32	34	36

Needle 2 will not be used for a while, and the stitches on Needles 3 and 4 are ignored while you knit the heel on Needle 1.

2. All of the heel stitches are worked in a slipped stitch rib pattern. This makes the heel thicker and stronger than the rest of the sock.

3. Row 1: *slip the first stitch (without knitting it), then knit the second stitch; repeat from * to the end of the needle.

4. Row 2: turn, slip the first stitch, then purl remainder of heel stitches to the end.

5. Repeat Steps 3 and 4 until you have worked as many rows as there are heel stitches, for example, if you have 32 sts for your heel, then you will work a total of 32 rows.

Heel stitches	28	30	32	34	36
Heel rows	28	30	32	34	36

You will notice on your heel that the slipped stitches create neat columns that provide a ridged texture, as well as creating a thick, strong fabric to help prevent your heel from wearing through.

It is important to maintain the 2-row slipped stitch pattern while you turn the heel, even though this will mean that sometimes there may be 2 slipped stitches next to each other. This won't be noticeable, due to the decreasing that will take place.

PART B – THE HEEL FLAP (FOR LEFT FOOT)

1. When the leg is completed, and the final round has been worked, knit across all of the stitches on Needles 1 and 2, then stop and slide all of the stitches from Needle 4 onto Needle 3.

These are now the heel stitches and they account for half of your total socks stitches.

The number of heel stitches now on Needle 3 for each size, are listed below:

Sock stitches	56	60	64	68	72
Heel stitches	28	30	32	34	36

Needle 4 will not be used for a while, and the stitches on Needles 1 and 2 are ignored whilst you knit the heel on Needle 3.

2. Now work as given for The Heel Flap (for the Right Foot) from Step 2 to the end.

VARIATION – FLAT HEEL

For the right foot, follow all of Step 4a, bullet point 1, to set up your heel. Needle 1 now holds the live stitches for the heel (as per table on page 120). Work on these stitches only.

1. Row 1 (RS): slip the first stitch then knit to the last 3 sts on Needle 1, k2tog, k1, turn.

2. Row 2: slip the first stitch then purl to the last 3 sts, p2tog, p1, turn.

3. Repeat these two rows until 12 stitches remain. For the second half of the heel you will pick up the slipped stitch from the beginning of each previous row, as follows:

4. Row 1 (RS): slip the first stitch then knit to the end, pick up and knit the slipped stitch from next row of first half, turn.

5. Row 2: slip the first stitch then purl to the end, pick up and purl the next slipped stitch from first half, turn.

6. Repeat these two rows until you have the same amount of stitches on Needle 1 that you had originally. Split these stitches back over Needles 1 and 2 and continue according to the foot pattern (noting that you do not work a gusset/instep with this type of heel).

7. Work as above for left foot, following all of Step 4b, bullet point 1, to set up your heel.

STEP 5 – TURNING THE HEEL (FOR BOTH FEET)

1. For all sizes, turn the heel as follows and continue to work in the 2-row slip stitch pattern throughout. For each part of the instruction, choose your size according to the original number of ankle stitches: 56 [60] [64] [68] [72] sts.

Slip the first stitch, pattern the next 16 [17] [18] [19] [21] sts, slip the next stitch, knit the next stitch, then pass the slipped stitch over the knitted stitch to decrease 1 stitch (⊿).

2. Turn the knitting, leaving the last 9 [10] [11] [12] [12] sts unworked. Slip the first stitch, purl 6 [6] [6] [6] [8] sts, then purl 2 sts together to decrease 1 stitch (⊿). Turn work.

You will now have 9 [10] [11] [12] [12] sts on each side of your decreases. Note that after each decreased stitch, there is a small, visible gap in your knitting. On each subsequent row you will work the 2 sts on each side of the gap together, to decrease another stitch, and this will close the gap.

3. For the next row, slip the first stitch, pattern until the decreased stitch is the next stitch, slip the next stitch, knit the next stitch, then pass the slipped stitch over the knitted stitch to decrease another stitch (⊿). Turn work.

4. For the next row, slip the first stitch then purl until the decreased stitch is the next stitch, then purl 2 sts together to decrease 1 stitch (⊿). Turn work.

You will now have 8 [9] [10] [11] [11] sts on each side of your decreases, plus the stitches in the centre. You will continue to decrease in this way (as stated in Step 5, point 2), working the two stitches on either side of the gap together until all of the heel stitches are used up.

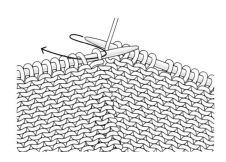

5. Repeat the last 2 rows (Steps 3 and 4) until you have no stitches left on either side of your decreases.

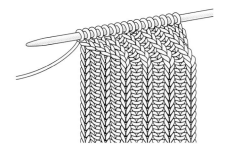

STEP 6 – THE INSTEP/GUSSET

You will now pick up stitches along the sides of the heel flap, from the slipped stitches that you made at the start of each of the heel flap rows, working from right to left. When picking up these stitches, it is important to insert your needle under both the loops of the stitch (and not just under one loop) as this will ensure a neat line and avoid making unsightly holes in your work.

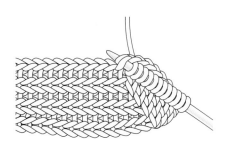

1. Continuing with working yarn and spare needle (now called Needle 1), knit across the 8 [8] [8] [8] [10] heel sts.

2. Pick up and knit 14 [15] [16] [17] [18] sts along the edge of the first heel flap.

3. To avoid a visible gap before the stitches on next needle, pick up and knit 1 extra stitch.

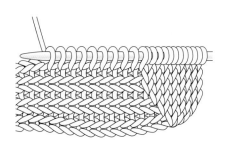

4. With Needle 2, knit across the stitches on the next needle.

5. With Needle 3, knit across the stitches on the next needle.

6. With Needle 4, pick up and knit 1 stitch directly after the stitches just worked (to avoid a visible gap before the heel), then pick up and knit 14 [15] [16] [17] [18] sts along the edge of the second heel flap

7. Knit 4 [4] [4] [4] [5] of the heel sts again so that the end of round finishes at centre of heel.

8. You should now have 64 [68] [72] [78] [82] sts, distributed as follows:

Original stitch count at ankle	56	60	64	68	72
Instep stitches	64	68	72	78	82
Stitches on Needles 1 and 4	18	19	20	22	23
Stitches on Needles 2 and 3	14	15	16	17	18

Now work a decrease round as follows:

9. Knit to last 3 sts on Needle 1, slip 1 stitch, knit 1 stitch, pass slipped stitch over the knitted stitch to decrease 1 st (◣).

10. Knit across all sts on Needles 2 and 3.

11. Knit first stitch on Needle 4, knit 2 sts together to decrease 1 st (◢), then knit to end.

12. Knit a full round without decreasing.

13. Repeat the last 2 rounds, following Steps 9–12, until you have decreased to the same number of stitches that you had before you started your heel.

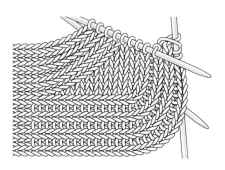

STEP 7 – FINISH THE FOOT

To finish the foot, work in stocking stitch for as many rounds as needed to reach halfway up your smallest toe (in line with the base of your big toe).

Count how many rounds you have worked so far, and make a note so that you can knit the second sock to match this.

STEP 8

OPTION 1 - ROUNDED TOE CAP AND FINISHING

The rounded toe is worked in stocking stitch and decreases are worked at the centre and end of each needle.

1. With 56 [60] [64] [68] [72] sts (14 [15] [16] [17] [18] sts per needle), *k5 [5] [6] [6] [7], k2tog (△), knit to last 2 stitches on needle, k2tog (△); rep from * on each needle to end of round, therefore decreasing 8 sts in total. Work 5 [5] [6] [6] [7] rounds straight.

2. Next round: *k4 [4] [5] [5] [6], k2tog △), knit to last 2 sts on needle, k2tog (△); rep from * to end of round. Work 4 [4] [5] [5] [6] rounds straight.

3. Next round: *k3 [3] [4] [4] [5], k2tog △), knit to last 2 sts on needle, k2tog (△); rep from * to end of round. Work 3 [3] [4] [5] [6] rounds straight.

4. Continue as given in Step 3, working 1 stitch less before each decrease on every decreasing round, until you have 8 sts remaining in total.

5. Cut yarn, leaving a long tail. Thread onto a tapestry needle, take the thread through the stitches and pull the yarn tail through to the wrong side, then secure with a few stitches.

6. Weave in ends to wrong side and trim.

OPTION 2 - BANDED TOE CAP AND FINISHING

The banded toe is worked in stocking stitch and decreases are worked at the end of the first and third needle and at the beginning of the second and fourth needle.

1. Knit across the stitches on Needle 1. This is now the new start of the round, and therefore the next needle will become Needle 1. You can mark this new start of the round, if desired, with a stitch marker or spare yarn.

2. Decrease round: on the first and third needle, work to last 3 sts, k2tog (△), knit last stitch. On the second and fourth needle, knit first stitch, slip next stitch knitwise, knit next stitch and pass slipped stitch over knitted stitch (◹). 52 [56] [60] [64] [68] sts.

3. Repeat the decrease round 2 [2] [3] [4] [5] times more. 44 [48] [48] [48] [48] sts.

4. Work 1 round straight, then repeat the decrease round. 40 [44] [44] [44] [44] sts.

5. Repeat last 2 rounds until 8 [12] [12] [12] [12] sts remain.

6. Cut yarn, leaving a long tail. Thread onto a tapestry needle, take the thread through the stitches and pull the yarn tail through to the wrong side, then secure with a few stitches.

7. Weave in ends to wrong side and trim.

Option 1

Option 2

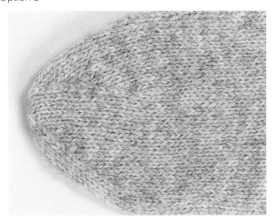

CUFF TECHNIQUES

THE NOTCHES

1. Work 5 rounds (or as many rounds as stated in the pattern) in knit stitch.

2. Knit 1 round according to the instructions below:

[K2tog, yo] to the end (△).

Note that the 'yo' creates a hole in your knitting. This round is the foldline.

3. Work a further 5 rounds (or as many rounds as stated in the pattern) in knit stitch.

4. Fold your knitting at the foldline, bringing the cast-on edge up at the back of your needles to meet the working edge.

5. For the next round, knit together one stitch from the left needle with one stitch from the cast-on edge of the knitting, making sure that these stitches are in line with each other. To do this, insert the right needle into the corresponding stitch along the cast-on edge.

Place this stitch on the tip of the left needle. Knit this stitch and the next stitch together as one stitch. Repeat this process for the remainder of the round, to complete the notches cuff.

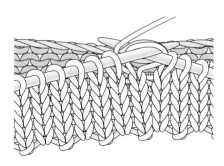

The notches cuff is represented on a chart as follows:

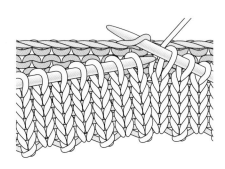

GARTER STITCH CUFF

After casting on, purl the first round, knit the second round, purl the third round and knit the fourth round. Then start knitting according to the pattern.

The garter stitch cuff is represented on a chart as follows:

LATVIAN BRAID

Knitted using two colours, over three rounds.

1. Choose one colour for A and another for B.

2. Knit the first round as follows: *k1 with A, k1 with B; repeat from * to the end of round.

3. Bring both yarns forward between needles to the front of the work.

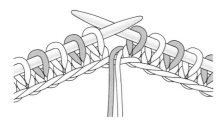

4. Purl the second round in the same colour sequence: *p1 with A, p1 with B; repeat from * to end of round and each time bring the next colour over the yarn you have just knitted with, to create the braiding effect.

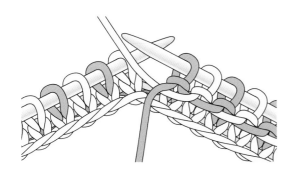

5. To create a Latvian Braid, repeat Step. 4 but each time pass the new yarn **under** the yarn you have just knitted with.

6. Take both yarns between the needles to the back of the work. Knit one row in the base colour of the pattern and then continue to follow the chart pattern.

The Latvian braid is represented on a chart as follows:

STRANDING YARN

When you are working with one or more strands of yarn at a time it is important to keep the balls of yarn separated, so that they do not become tangled. It helps if you can place one ball of yarn on your right and one ball of yarn on your left.

Always carry the yarn not being used loosely across the back of your work until you need it next and don't pull it too tightly, otherwise your knitting will pucker.

When changing colour, always choose one colour that will feed in to your knitting above the other colour (from the top) and feed the other colour in from the bottom. If you maintain this order throughout your knitting, your Fair Isle patterning will look uniform and neat.

BLOCKING YOUR PROJECTS

Once you have finished your socks, stockings or leg warmers, it is recommended to block them to even out the stitches. Spray one side of the knitting with cold water until wet, but not saturated. Gently press the water into the stitches with your hands, then pin out flat to dry or place over sock blockers. If you feel that your socks need stretching slightly to fit, pin to the desired size and leave to dry.

ABOUT THE AUTHOR

Ieva Ozolina is the founder and creator of the 'Knit like a Latvian' brand of knitting kits and books. Ieva started knitting when she was 14 and has been passionate about knitting ever since.

Ieva has represented her knitting kits at more than 40 international shows and exhibitions to spread her love for Latvian socks, mittens and other Latvian knitting traditions all over the world.

In 2009 she, together with her husband Maris, started a knitting and yarn company Hobbywool.

Ieva lives in Riga, the capital of Latvia, a beautiful UNESCO pearl. That is also where you'll find her wool concept store Hobbywool.

You are always welcome to visit!

REFERENCES

Ģibiete, Lia Mona (2017). Suitu rakstainās zeķes. Latvijas Nacionālais kultūras centrs

Jansone, Aija (2008). Dzīvā cimdu un zeķu adīšanas tradīcija Vārkavā. Riga, Latvia: Zinātne

Jansone, Aija (2011). Rucavas rakstaino adījumu mantojums. Riga, Latvia: Zinātne

Karnups Adolfs (1939). Novadu tērpi. Jelgava, Latvia: Latvijas pilsētu savienības izdevums

Slava, Mirdza (1990).Latviešu rakstainie cimdi. Riga, Latvia: Zinātne

Latvijas Vēstures Muzejs (1995-1997-2003). Latviešu tautas tērpi (three books). Riga, Latvia: Latvijas Nacionālais Vēstures Muzejs

OTHER SOURCES

The Ethnographic open-air museum of Latvia (EBM)

Madona Local History and Art Museum (MNM)

Kuldiga District Museum (KNM)

Liepaja Museum (LM)

Thank You

First of all, I want to thank all Latvian women, who have knitted for centuries, keeping our traditions alive and leaving us with the most beautiful heritage of patterns.

I want to thank Sarah Callard, Commissioning Editor, who offered me the opportunity to write this book.

A special thanks to Betija Markusa, who made the pattern drawings and has been the biggest help in creating this book.

Thanks to Dr. Hist. Aija Jansone, whose books and wide knowledge of Latvian mittens and knitting traditions inspired me to make my own knitting kits as well as to write this book.

Thanks to Lia Mona Gibiete for inspiration and advice for the Suiti socks knitting techniques.

Thanks to Jolanta Medina from Kuldiga District Museum for all the help.

Thanks to Sandra Lipska, Lubov Yakimova, Henisa Silina, Zinta Blanka, Solvita Cipruse, Dina Gravite, Sigita Lielpetere and Inta Zile for help with all the knitting.

Thanks to Hobbywool team member Iveta Kulina for all the help throughout the creation of this book.

And last but not least, a BIG thanks to my dear family for all the support.

INDEX

SUPPLIERS

Hobbywool 2-ply 100% wool yarns are made in Latvia and are the perfect choice for sock and mitten knitting. All yarns are made from pure, natural fibres and at Hobbywool you will find a wide range of colours – from earth tones to bright colours.

All Hobbywool yarns and knitting equipment can be purchased direct from:

www.hobbywool.com

A DAVID AND CHARLES BOOK
© David and Charles, Ltd 2019

David and Charles is an imprint of David and Charles, Ltd
1 Emperor Way, Exeter Business Park, Exeter, EX1 3QS

Text and Designs © Ieva Ozolina 2019
Layout and Photography © David and Charles, Ltd 2019

First published in the UK and USA in 2019

Ieva Ozolina has asserted her right to be identified as author of this work in accordance with the Copyright, Designs and Patents Act, 1988.

The author and publisher have made every effort to ensure that all the instructions in the book are accurate and safe, and therefore cannot accept liability for any resulting injury, damage or loss to persons or property, however it may arise.

Names of manufacturers and product ranges are provided for the information of readers, with no intention to infringe copyright or trademarks.

A catalogue record for this book is available from the British Library.

ISBN-13: 9781446307496 paperback
ISBN-13: 9781446378779 EPUB

Printed in Slovenia by GPS Group for:
David and Charles, Ltd
1 Emperor Way, Exeter Business Park, Exeter, EX1 3QS

10 9 8 7 6 5 4 3 2 1

Content Director: Ame Verso
Senior Commissioning Editor: Sarah Callard
Managing Editor: Jeni Hennah
Project Editors: Lynne Rowe and Neti Love
Design Manager: Anna Wade
Designers: Prudence Rogers and Ali Stark
Photographer: Jason Jenkins
Art Director: Prudence Rogers
Illustrator: Kuo Kang Chen
Production Manager: Beverley Richardson

David and Charles publishes high-quality books on a wide range of subjects.
For more information visit www.davidandcharles.com.

Layout of the digital edition of this book may vary depending on reader hardware and display settings.